ORDINARY DIFFERENTIAL EQUATIONS

Systems, Discrete Models and Chaos

William Dean Stone

New Mexico Tech

Linus
Publications, Inc.

Published by Linus Publications, Inc.

Deer Park, NY 11729

ISBN 1-934188-74-3

Printed in the United States of America.

10 9 8 7 6 5 4 3 2 1

Table of Contents

PART I

FIRST ORDER LINEAR ORDINARY DIFFERENTIAL EQUATIONS

CHAPTER

Preliminaries

In the study of differential equations, one of the first problems one looks at is

$$\frac{dx}{dt} = ax, x(0) = x_0 \tag{1.1}$$

where x is a scalar valued function of the independent variable t; a and x_0 are constants. This equation arises in a variety of contexts, including bacterial growth and radioactive decay, where the rate of change of a quantity is proportional to the amount. The equation (1.1) can be readily solved by separation of variables:

$$\frac{dx}{x} = adt$$

$$\ln|x| = at + c$$

$$x = ke^{at}, (k = \pm e^c).$$

The initial condition, $x(0) = x_0$, leads to $x(0) = ke^{a0} = k = x_0$ so a solution to the initial value problem (2.1) is given by:

$$x(t) = x_0 e^{at}. \tag{1.2}$$

In situations where the rate of change of x depends not only on the amount of x, but also on some external effects, we have a nonhomogeneous equation that is an equation of the form

$$\frac{dx}{dt} = ax + r(t), x(0) = x_0. \tag{1.3}$$

The method for solving (1.3) depends on the form of $r(t)$. For many nice $r(t)s$ we can use the method of undetermined coefficients.

Undetermined coefficients: If $\left\{ r(t), \dfrac{dr}{dt}, \dfrac{d^2r}{dt^2}, \dfrac{d^3r}{dt^3}, \cdots \right\}$ can be spanned by the finite set of linearly independent functions $(\phi_1(t), \phi_2(t), \cdots, \phi_k(t))$ then form the linear combination

$$a_1\phi_1(t) + a_2\phi_2(t) + \cdots + a_k\phi_k(t). \tag{1.4}$$

Substitute (1.4) in for x in (1.3) and equate coefficients of $\phi_j(t)$ on both sides. This leads to a linear system of algebraic equations that can be solved, giving a particular solution, x_p, to the equation (1.3).

If we take this particular solution plus a general solution to the homogeneous problem (1.1), we get $Ae^{at} + x_p(t)$, a general solution to (1.3). The condition $x(0) = x_0$ can be used to solve for A:

$$x_o = x(0) = Ae^{a0} + x_p(0) = A + x_p(0) \text{ so } A = x_0 - x_p(0)$$

and

$$x(t) = (x_0 - x_p(0))e^{at} + x_p(t). \tag{1.5}$$

For example, if we want to solve $\dfrac{dx}{dt} = 2x + t^2$ then $r(t) = t^2$ and the set of r and all its derivatives $\{t^2, 2t, 2, 0, 0 \cdots\}$ is spanned by $\{t^2, t, 1\}$. We look for x_p in the form $at^2 + bt + c$. Thus $\dfrac{dx}{dt} = 2at + b$ and we get $2at + b = 2at^2 + 2bt + 2c + t^2$. Equating coefficients we get:

$$0 = 2a + 1 \qquad a = -\frac{1}{2}$$

$$2a = 2b \quad \Rightarrow \quad b = -\frac{1}{2}$$

$$b = 2c \qquad c = -\frac{1}{4}$$

so $x_p = -\dfrac{1}{2}t^2 - \dfrac{1}{2}t - \dfrac{1}{4}$, and anything of the form $Ae^{2t} - \dfrac{1}{2}t^2 - \dfrac{1}{2}t - \dfrac{1}{4}$ is a solution to our problem; A can be chosen to be $x_0 + \dfrac{1}{4}$ to match initial conditions.

Sometimes the method has to be modified. If one of the ϕs is itself a solution to the homogeneous equation or a power of t times such a solution, it must be replaced by t times what it was. For instance, consider the problem

$$\frac{dx}{dt} = -x + e^{-t} + \cos t. \tag{1.6}$$

The method of undetermined coefficients gives the guess

$$x_p = ae^{-t} + b\cos t + c\sin t \tag{1.7}$$

but this leads to a system of algebraic equations with no solution.

The problem is that e^{-t} is a solution to $\frac{dx}{dt} = -x$. The modification rule gives the guess

$$x_p = ate^{-t} + b\cos t + c\sin t \tag{1.8}$$

which works.

In some situations we have an equation involving higher order derivatives of $x(t)$. This is the main topic in a first course in differential equations. In other cases, we might have an unknown function of several variables. This is covered in partial differential equations.

We wish to consider yet another generalization of our basic problem. Suppose we have several unknown functions, all dependent on the same independent variable. Now instead of a single equation, we will have a system of equations for these dependent variables. If we can solve for the growth rates of each of these unknowns in terms of the functions and the dependent variable t, we will have a system of first order equations.

Clearly, if the rates of change of the various quantities are independent of the other quantities, everything is easy. The system in uncoupled (the derivatives of one dependent variable does not depend on any of the other dependent variables). Each equation can be solved separately; what we have is not really a system of equations, but a list of equations, all independent. For example:

$$\frac{dx_1}{dt} = x_1$$

$$\frac{dx_2}{dt} = -3x_2$$

with $x_1(0) = 2, x_2(0) = 4$ leads to $x_1(t) = -2e^t, x_2(t) = 4e^{-3t}$.

If, however, the equations are coupled, the results are not so simple. For instance, consider the system

$$\frac{dx_1}{dt} = -2x_1 - x_2, x_1(0) = 1$$

$$\frac{dx_2}{dt} = -x_1 - 2x_2, x_2(0) = 3. \tag{1.9}$$

No simple separation of variables appears to work. This will be our topic for the next several chapters.

Exercises

1.1   Consider the nonhomogeneous equation (1.3) with $r(t)$ a constant:

$$\frac{dx}{dt} = ax + b, x(0) = x_0$$

This could, of course, be solved by undetermined coefficients, but it can also be solved by separation of variables. Solve by separation of variables.

1.2   Substitute (1.7) into (1.6) and show that it doesn't work.

1.3   Solve (1.6) with $x(0) = 3$.

Substitution

There are many ways to solve coupled systems of equations such as the one at the end of the previous chapter (1.9). One of the simplest conceptually is the method of substitution. For this method we eliminate one of the dependent variables and then solve the remaining second order equation in one dependent variable. If we have

$$\frac{dx_1}{dt} = a_{11}x_1 + a_{12}x_2$$

$$\frac{dx_2}{dt} = a_{21}x_1 + a_{22}x_2 \tag{2.1}$$

we can solve the first equation for x_2 (assuming $a_{12} \neq 0$). We get

$$x_2 = \frac{1}{a_{12}} \frac{dx_1}{dt} - \frac{a_{11}}{a_{12}} x_1. \tag{2.2}$$

Differentiating this with respect to t gives

$$\frac{dx_2}{dt} = \frac{1}{a_{12}} \frac{d^2x_1}{dt^2} - \frac{a_{11}}{a_{12}} \frac{dx_1}{dt}. \tag{2.3}$$

Substituting the expressions (2.2), (2.3) into the second equation of (2.1) yields

$$\frac{1}{a_{12}} \frac{d^2x_1}{dt^2} - \frac{a_{11}}{a_{12}} \frac{dx_1}{dt} = a_{21}x_1 + \frac{a_{22}}{a_{12}} \frac{dx_1}{dt} - \frac{a_{11}a_{22}}{a_{12}} x_1$$

or

$$\frac{1}{a_{12}} \frac{d^2x_1}{dt^2} - \left(\frac{a_{11}}{a_{12}} + \frac{a_{22}}{a_{12}} \right) \frac{dx_1}{dt} + \left(\frac{a_{11}a_{22}}{a_{12}} - a_{21} \right) x_1 = 0$$

This is a second order linear differential equation for x_1. Solve this and substitute the result into equation (2.2) to get x_2. Initial conditions may then be satisfied. As an illustration, consider our example (1.9).

$$\frac{dx_1}{dt} = -2x_1 - x_2, \; x_1(0) = 1$$

$$\frac{dx_2}{dt} = -x_1 - 2x_2, \; x_2(0) = 3 \tag{2.4}$$

Solving for x_2 gives

$$x_2 = -\frac{dx_1}{dt} - 2x_1,$$

so

$$\frac{dx_2}{dt} = -\frac{d^2x_1}{dt^2} - 2\frac{dx_1}{dt}.$$

Substituting these in yields

$$\frac{d^2x_1}{dt^2} + \frac{dx_1}{dt} + 3x_1 = 0.$$

Letting $x_1 = e^{\lambda t}$ gives $\lambda^2 + 4\lambda + 3 = 0$, so $\lambda = -3$ or -1, and we get

$$x_1 = Ae^{-t} + Be^{-3t}.$$

Thus, $\dfrac{dx_1}{dt} = -Ae^{-t} - 3Be^{-3t}$ and $x_2 = -\left(-Ae^{-t} - 3Be^{-3t}\right) - 2\left(Ae^{-t} + Be^{-3t}\right) = -Ae^{-t} + Be^{-3t}$. Now $x_1(0) = Ae^{-0} + Be^{-3(0)} = A + B = 1$, and $x(0) = -Ae^{-0} + Be^{-3(0)} = -A + B = 3$, so $A = -1, B = 2$, and we get the solution

$$x_1(t) = -e^{-t} + 2e^{-3t}$$

$$x_2(t) = e^{-t} + 2e^{-3t}. \tag{2.5}$$

We can easily plug (2.5) back into (2.4) to verify that it is a solution.

EXERCISES

2.1   Verify that (2.5) is a solution to the initial value problem (2.4).

2.2   What happens in (2.1) if a_{12} is zero? Consider the equation

$$\frac{dx_1}{dt} = -3x_1, \, x_1(0) = 1$$

$$\frac{dx_2}{dt} = x_1 - 2x_2, \, x_2(0) = 2.$$

Solve it two ways:

(a)   Solve the first equation and plug the result into the second.

(b)   *Solve (algebraically) the second equation for x_1 and substitute the result into the first equation.*

Solve the following initial value problems.

2.3 $$\frac{dx_1}{dt} = -3x_1 - x_2, \, x_1(0) = 1$$

$$\frac{dx_2}{dt} = -2x_1 - 2x_2, \, x_2(0) = -2.$$

2.4 $$\frac{dx_1}{dt} = -x_1 - x_2, \, x_1(0) = 0$$

$$\frac{dx_2}{dt} = x_1 - 3x_2, \, x_2(0) = 1.$$

2.5 $$\frac{dx_1}{dt} = x_2, \, x_1(0) = 1$$

$$\frac{dx_2}{dt} = -x_1, \, x_2(0) = -1.$$

2.6 $$\frac{dx_1}{dt} = -x_1 + x_2, \, x_1(0) = 1$$

$$\frac{dx_2}{dt} = -x_1 - x_2, \, x_2(0) = 2.$$

The method in this section will also work for nonhomogeneous systems. Try the following, using the same steps: solve for x_2, get $\frac{dx_2}{dt}$, plug them in, solve for x_1, get x_2.

2.7 $\dfrac{dx_1}{dt} = -3x_1 - x_2 + 5,\ x_1(0) = 3$

$\dfrac{dx_2}{dt} = -2x_1 - 2x_2 + 2,\ x_2(0) = 0.$

2.8 $\dfrac{dx_1}{dt} = x_2 + 1,\ x_1(0) = 0$

$\dfrac{dx_2}{dt} = -x_1 + 2,\ x_2(0) = 1.$

The method even works if the nonhomogeneity is not a constant. The resulting uncoupled system will also have nonconstant nonhomogeneities and will have to be solved by the method of undetermined coefficients (if applicable) or variation of parameters. For example, consider

$$\dfrac{dx}{dt} = x + y + e^{2t},\ x(0) = 0$$

$$\dfrac{dy}{dt} = 4x + y - t,\ x(0) = 1 \tag{2.6}$$

Solving the first for y gives $y = \dfrac{dx}{dt} - x - e^{2t}$ so $\dfrac{dy}{dt} = \dfrac{d^2x}{dt^2} - \dfrac{dx}{dt} - 2e^{2t}$ and the second

equation becomes $\dfrac{d^2x}{dt^2} - \dfrac{dx}{dt} - 2e^{2t} = 4x + \dfrac{dx}{dt} - x - e^{2t} - t$ or

$$\dfrac{d^2x}{dt^2} - 2\dfrac{dx}{dt} - 3x = e^{2t} - t \tag{2.7}$$

We guess a solution to the homogeneous of $x = e^{\lambda t}$. This gives

$$\lambda^2 - 2\lambda - 3 = 0 \tag{2.8}$$

so $\lambda = 3$ or $=1$ and $x_h(t)\quad Ae^{3t} + Be^{-t}$. The method of undetermined coefficients

gives $x_p = ae^{2t} + bt + c$. Substituting this into equation (2.7) gives

$$4ae^{2t} - 2(2ae^{2t} + b) - 3\left(ae^{2t} + bt + c\right) = e^{2t} - t \tag{2.9}$$

or, equating coefficients,

$$-3a = 1$$

$$-3b = -1$$

$$-2b - 3c = 0 \tag{2.10}$$

so

$$a = -\frac{1}{3}, b = \frac{1}{3}, c = -\frac{2}{9} \text{ and } x_p = -\frac{1}{3}e^{2t} + \frac{1}{3}t - \frac{2}{9} \text{ and}$$

$$x = Ae^{3t} + Be^{-t} - \frac{1}{3}e^{2t} + \frac{1}{3}t - \frac{2}{9} \tag{2.11}$$

We know

$$y = \frac{dx}{dt} - x - e^{2t} = 3Ae^{3t} - Be^{-t} - \frac{2}{3}e^{2t} + \frac{1}{3} - Ae^{3t} - Be^{-t} = \frac{1}{3}e^{2t} - \frac{1}{3}t + \frac{2}{9} - e^{2t}$$

so

$$y = 2Ae^{3t} - 2Be^{-t} - \frac{4}{3}e^{2t} - \frac{1}{3}t + \frac{5}{9} \tag{2.12}$$

Initial conditions give

$$x(0) = A + B - \frac{1}{3} - \frac{2}{9} = A + B - \frac{5}{9} = x_0 = 0$$

$$y(0) = 2A - 2B - \frac{4}{3} + \frac{5}{9} = 2A - 2B - \frac{7}{9} = y_0 = 1. \tag{2.13}$$

This gives $A = \frac{13}{18}, B = \frac{1}{6}$ and, finally,

$$x(t) = \frac{13}{18}e^{3t} + \frac{1}{6}e^{-t} - \frac{1}{3}e^{2t} + \frac{1}{3}t - \frac{2}{9}$$

$$y(t) = \frac{13}{9}e^{3t} - \frac{1}{3}e^{-t} - \frac{4}{3}e^{2t} - \frac{1}{3}t + \frac{5}{9} \tag{2.14}$$

Try this with:

2.9 $\quad \dfrac{dx_1}{dt} = -2x_1 - x_2 + e^{-2t}, x_1(0) = 1$

$\quad \dfrac{dx_2}{dt} = -x_1 - 2x_2 + t, x_2(0) = 0.$

CHAPTER

Eigenvector Methods

Another technique for solving systems of linear equations is based on the eigenvalues and eigenvectors of a matrix. This more geometric approach will be important when we get to nonlinear systems. Consider the system (2.1). Written in matrix, vector form it becomes

$$\frac{dx}{dt} = Ax, \tag{3.1}$$

where $x(t) = \begin{pmatrix} x_1(t) \\ x_2(t) \end{pmatrix}, A = \begin{pmatrix} a_{11} & a_{12} \\ a_{21} & a_{22} \end{pmatrix}$. If initial conditions are given they would be

in the form $x(0) = \begin{pmatrix} x_1(0) \\ x_2(0) \end{pmatrix} = x_0$. Suppose the matrix A has two eigenvalues λ_1, λ_2

and two linearly independent eigenvectors u_1, u_2 such that $Au_1 = \lambda_1 u_1$. Since $\{u_1, u_2\}$ $\{u_1, u_2\}$ is linearly independent, it forms a basis for $\mathbb{R}^2$. Thus any vector can be written as a linear combination of u_1 and u_2. Set

$$x(t) = a_1(t)u_1 + a_2(t)u_2. \tag{3.2}$$

As x changes with time, the scalar coefficients a_1, a_2 will also change, but the basis elements u_1, u_2 are constant vectors. If we substitute (3.2) into (3.1) we get

$$\frac{d}{dt}(a_1(t)u_1 + a_2(t)u_2 =$$

$$\frac{da_1(t)}{dt}u_1 + \frac{da_2(t)}{dt}u_2 =$$

$$A(a_1(t) + a_2(t)u_2) =$$

$$A_1(t)\lambda_1 + a_2(t)\lambda_2 u_2.$$

This follows from the fact that u_1 and u_2 are constant, thus unaffected by differentiation, a_1, a_2 are scalars, thus they factor out of matrix multiplication, and u_1 and u_2 are eigenvectors of A. From this we get

$$\left[\frac{d}{dt}a_1(t) - \lambda_1 a_1(t)\right]u_1 + \left[\frac{d}{dt}a_2(t) - \lambda_2 a_2(t)\right]u_2 = 0.$$

Therefore, by independence of u_1 and u_2

$$\frac{da_1}{dt} = \lambda_1 a_1(t)$$

$$\frac{da_2(t)}{dt} = \lambda_2 a_2(t). \tag{3.3}$$

This new system (3.3) is uncoupled. We can easily solve and get

$$a_1(t) = k_1 e^{\lambda_1 t}, a_2(t) = k_2 e^{\lambda_2 t}. \tag{3.4}$$

If we have an initial condition $x(0) = x_0$, we write this in terms of the basis vectors, also:

$$x_0 = a_{10}u_1 + a_{20}u_2. \tag{3.5}$$

Thus, $x(0) = a_1(0)u_1 + a_2(0)u_2 = x_0 = a_{10}u_1 + a_{20}u_2$, and again by independence of u_1 and u_2, we get

$$a_1(0) = a_{10}, a_2(0) = a_{20} \tag{3.6}$$

initial conditions for $a_1(t)$ and $a_2(t)$. Now that we know $a_1(t)$ and $a_2(t)$, we get our original variables back by substituting into (3.2):

$$x(t) = \begin{pmatrix} x_1(t) \\ x_2(t) \end{pmatrix} = a_{10}e^{\lambda_1 t}u_1 + a_{20}e^{\lambda_2 t}u_2. \tag{3.7}$$

As an example, let us look again at system (2.4). Written in vector form we have

$$\frac{d}{dt}\begin{pmatrix} x_1 \\ x_2 \end{pmatrix} = \begin{pmatrix} -2 & -1 \\ -1 & -2 \end{pmatrix}\begin{pmatrix} x_1 \\ x_2 \end{pmatrix}, x_0 = \begin{pmatrix} 1 \\ 3 \end{pmatrix}. \tag{3.8}$$

To get the eigenvalues of A, set the determinant of $A - \lambda 1$ equal to zero:

$$det\,(A - \lambda I) = \begin{vmatrix} (-2 - \lambda) & -1 \\ -1 & (-2 - \lambda) \end{vmatrix} = (-2 - \lambda)^2 - 1 = \lambda^2 + 4\lambda + 3 = 0.$$

Thus, $\lambda = -1$ or -3. The kernel of $A+I$ is spanned by $\begin{pmatrix} 1 \\ -1 \end{pmatrix}$, the kernel of

$A+3I$ by $\begin{pmatrix} 1 \\ 1 \end{pmatrix}$. Let

$$x = a_1(t)\begin{pmatrix} +1 \\ -1 \end{pmatrix} + a_2(t)\begin{pmatrix} 1 \\ 1 \end{pmatrix}, \tag{3.9}$$

and write

$$x_0 = \begin{pmatrix} 1 \\ 3 \end{pmatrix} = -1\begin{pmatrix} 1 \\ -1 \end{pmatrix} + 2\begin{pmatrix} 1 \\ 1 \end{pmatrix}, \tag{3.10}$$

Equation (3.8) becomes

$$\frac{da_1}{dt}\begin{pmatrix} 1 \\ -1 \end{pmatrix} + \frac{da_2}{dt}\begin{pmatrix} 1 \\ 1 \end{pmatrix} = -a_1(t)\begin{pmatrix} 1 \\ -1 \end{pmatrix} - 3a_2(t)\begin{pmatrix} 1 \\ 1 \end{pmatrix},$$

$$a_1(0) = -1, a_2(0) = 2.$$

Equating coefficients on the basis elements, we get

$$\frac{da_1}{dt} = -a_1(t), \quad a_1(0) = -1$$

$$\frac{da_2}{dt} = -3a_2(t), a_2(0) = 2 \tag{3.11}$$

so $a_1(t) = -e^{-t}, a_2(t) = 2e^{-3t}$, and our solution is:

$$\begin{pmatrix} x_1(t) \\ x_2(t) \end{pmatrix} = -e^{-1}\begin{pmatrix} 1 \\ -1 \end{pmatrix} + 2e^{-3t}\begin{pmatrix} 1 \\ 1 \end{pmatrix}. \tag{3.12}$$

Compare this to our previous solution, (2.5). If the matrix A has two distinct real eigenvalues, this all goes through and (3.7) gives the solution. If the determinant of $A - \lambda I$ has complex roots, everything still works; (3.7) still gives the solution. Assuming A has real entries, complex roots must come in complex conjugate pairs. If $\lambda_2 = conj(\lambda_1)$, then $u_2 = conj(u_1)$. Also, if x_0 is real, then $a_{20} = conj(a_{10})$ and $a_2(t) = conj(a_1(t))$. The solutions will be real.

To write our solution in real form, we will need

$$e^{a+ib} = e^a \left(\cos b + i \sin b \right). \tag{3.13}$$

As an example we consider

$$\frac{dx_1}{dt} = - x_1 + x_2, x_1 \ (0) = 1$$

$$\frac{dx_2}{dt} = - x_1 - x_2, x_2(0) = 2,$$

or in matrix form

$$\frac{dx_1}{dt} = \begin{pmatrix} -1 & 1 \\ -1 & -1 \end{pmatrix} x, x(0) = \begin{pmatrix} 1 \\ 2 \end{pmatrix}. \tag{3.14}$$

The determinant of $A - \lambda I = (-1 - \lambda)^2 + 1 = \lambda^2 + 2\lambda + 2$ which has roots of

$\lambda = -1 \pm i$. For $\lambda = -1 + i, A - \lambda I = \begin{pmatrix} -i & 1 \\ -1 & -i \end{pmatrix}$ and the kernel is spanned by $\begin{pmatrix} 1 \\ i \end{pmatrix}$. For

$\lambda = -1 - i$ we get the kernel of $\begin{pmatrix} i & 1 \\ -1 & -i \end{pmatrix}$ spanned by $\begin{pmatrix} 1 \\ -i \end{pmatrix}$.

Actually, once we have u_1, since $\lambda_2 = conj(\lambda_1)$ we know $u_2 = conj(u_1)$.

Now let

$$x(0) = a_1(t) \begin{pmatrix} 1 \\ i \end{pmatrix} + a_2(t) \begin{pmatrix} 1 \\ -i \end{pmatrix}. \tag{3.15}$$

The initial condition becomes

$$x(0) = \begin{pmatrix} 1 \\ 2 \end{pmatrix} = \left(\frac{1}{2} - i \right) \begin{pmatrix} 1 \\ i \end{pmatrix} + \left(\frac{1}{2} + i \right) \begin{pmatrix} 1 \\ -i \end{pmatrix}, \tag{3.16}$$

and we get

$$\frac{da_1}{dt} \begin{pmatrix} 1 \\ i \end{pmatrix} + \frac{da_2}{dt} \begin{pmatrix} 1 \\ -i \end{pmatrix} = (-1+i) a_1(t) \begin{pmatrix} 1 \\ i \end{pmatrix} + (-1-i) a_2(t) \begin{pmatrix} 1 \\ i \end{pmatrix}$$

or

$$\frac{da_1}{dt} = (-1+i) a_1(t), a_1(0) = \frac{1}{2} - i$$

$$\frac{da_2}{dt} = (-1-i) a_2(t), a_2(0) = \frac{1}{2} + i. \tag{3.17}$$

Thus

$$a_1(t) = \left(\frac{1}{2} - i\right) e^{(-1+i)t}$$

$$a_2(t) = \left(\frac{1}{2} + i\right) e^{(-1-i)t}. \tag{3.18}$$

Using (3.13) we get

$$a_1(t) = \left(\frac{1}{2} - i\right) e^{-t}(\cos t + i \sin t)$$

$$a_2(t) = \left(\frac{1}{2} + i\right) e^{-t}(\cos t - i \sin t).$$

or

$$a_1(t) = e^{-t}\left[\left(\frac{1}{2}\cos t + \sin t\right) + \left(\frac{1}{2}\sin t - \cos t\right)i\right]$$

$$a_2(t) = e^{-t}\left[\left(\frac{1}{2}\cos t + \sin t\right) + \left(\cos t - \frac{1}{2}\sin t\right)i\right]$$

So,

$$x = a_1(t)\begin{pmatrix}1\\i\end{pmatrix} + a_2(t)\begin{pmatrix}1\\-i\end{pmatrix} = \begin{pmatrix}e^{-t}[\cos t + 2\sin t]\\e^{-t}[2\cos t - \sin t]\end{pmatrix} \tag{3.19}$$

Compare this to your solution for exercise 2.6.

Nonhomogeneous systems present no particular added difficulty. The nonhomogeneous term must be written in terms of the basis vectors, which then results in nonhomogeneous equations for $a_1(t), a_2(t)$. As an example consider:

$$\frac{dx}{dt} = \begin{pmatrix}-2 & -1\\-1 & -2\end{pmatrix}x + \begin{pmatrix}2\\1\end{pmatrix}, x(0) = \begin{pmatrix}1\\3\end{pmatrix}. \tag{3.20}$$

The matrix A is the same as in (3.8), so the eigenvalues and eigenvectors are again -1, $\begin{pmatrix}1\\-1\end{pmatrix}$ and -3, $\begin{pmatrix}1\\1\end{pmatrix}$. Write

$$\begin{pmatrix}2\\1\end{pmatrix} = \frac{3}{2}\begin{pmatrix}1\\1\end{pmatrix} + \frac{1}{2}\begin{pmatrix}1\\-1\end{pmatrix}. \tag{3.21}$$

As before $\begin{pmatrix} 1 \\ 3 \end{pmatrix} = 2\begin{pmatrix} 1 \\ 1 \end{pmatrix} - \begin{pmatrix} 1 \\ -1 \end{pmatrix}$ and we let $x = a_1(t)\begin{pmatrix} 1 \\ -1 \end{pmatrix} + a_2(t)\begin{pmatrix} 1 \\ 1 \end{pmatrix}$.

Substituting this all into (3.20) and equating coefficients on the basis vectors gives

$$\frac{da_1}{dt} = -a_1(t) + \frac{1}{2}, a_1(0) = -1$$

$$\frac{da_2}{dt} = -3a_2(t) + \frac{3}{2}, a_2(0) = 2. \tag{3.22}$$

Using undetermined coefficients, we get

$$a_1(t) = -\frac{3}{2}e^{-t} + \frac{1}{2}$$

$$a_2(t) = \frac{3}{2}e^{-3t} + \frac{1}{2} \tag{3.23}$$

or

$$\begin{pmatrix} x_1(t) \\ x_2(t) \end{pmatrix} = \left(-\frac{3}{2}e^{-t} + \frac{1}{2}\right)\begin{pmatrix} 1 \\ -1 \end{pmatrix} + \left(\frac{3}{2}e^{-3t} + \frac{1}{2}\right)\begin{pmatrix} 1 \\ 1 \end{pmatrix}$$

$$= \begin{pmatrix} -\dfrac{3}{2}e^{-t} + \dfrac{3}{2}e^{-3t} + 1 \\ \dfrac{3}{2}e^{-t} + \dfrac{3}{2}e^{-3t} \end{pmatrix}. \tag{3.24}$$

This technique of writing everything in terms of the eigenvectors is equivalent to a change of basis. If A, an $n \times n$ matrix, is diagonable, i.e. it has n linearly independent eigenvectors, then there is an invertible matrix p such that $P^{-1}AP = D$ where $D = diag(\lambda_1, \lambda_2, \cdots, \lambda_n)$. Thus $A = PDP^{-1}$. Consider then, a system of linear differential equations:

$$\frac{dx}{dt} = Ax + b(t), \ x(0) = x_0. \tag{3.25}$$

If A is a constant, diagonable matrix, we can write

$$\frac{dx}{dt} = PDP^{-1}x + b, x(0) = x_0$$

or, multiplying on the left by P^{-1},

$$P^{-1}\frac{dx}{dt} = DP^{-1}x + P^{-1}b, P^{-1}x(0) = P^{-1}x_0.$$

If A is constant, P^{-1} will be also. Thus:

$$\frac{d}{dt}(P^{-1}x) = D(P^{-1}x) + P^{-1}b(t), P^{-1}x(0) = P^{-1}x_0. \qquad (3.26)$$

$P^{-1}b(t)$ is a known vector function of t, call it $b*(t)$; $P^{-1}x_0$ is a known constant vector, call it y_0. Let the unknown vector function $P^{-1}x(t)$ be called $y(t)$. Now we have

$$\frac{dy}{dt} = Dy + b^*(t), y(0) = y_0 \qquad (3.27)$$

This is a diagonal (uncoupled) system and can thus be readily solved.

EXERCISES

3.1 Verify that the values for x_1 and x_2 in equation (3.24) are solutions to the initial value problem (3.20).

Using the techniques in this section redo:

3.2 Exercise #2.3

3.3 Exercise #2.5

3.4 Why can't #2.4 be done using the techniques in this section?

3.5 Exercise #2.7

3.6 Exercise #2.8

Non-constant nonhomogeneities can also be dealt with. One way to compute the coefficients of u_1, u_2, is to first write $\begin{pmatrix}1\\0\end{pmatrix}$ and $\begin{pmatrix}0\\1\end{pmatrix}$ in terms u_1 and u_2. For instance, if

$u_1 = \begin{pmatrix}1\\-1\end{pmatrix}$ and $u_2 = \begin{pmatrix}1\\1\end{pmatrix}$ then $\begin{pmatrix}1\\0\end{pmatrix} = \frac{1}{2}u_1 + \frac{1}{2}u_2$ and $\begin{pmatrix}0\\1\end{pmatrix} = -\frac{1}{2}u_1 + \frac{1}{2}u_2$. Thus

$$\begin{pmatrix}t\\e^{-t}\end{pmatrix} = t\begin{pmatrix}1\\0\end{pmatrix} + e^{-t}\begin{pmatrix}0\\1\end{pmatrix} = t\left(\frac{1}{2}u_1 + \frac{1}{2}u_2\right) + e^{-t}\left(-\frac{1}{2}u_1 + \frac{1}{2}u_2\right) = \left(\frac{t}{2} - \frac{e^{-t}}{2}\right)u_1 + \left(\frac{t}{2} + \frac{e^{-t}}{2}\right)u_2.$$

3.7   Solve
$$\frac{dx_1}{dt} = -2x_1 + x_2 + t, \ x_1(0) = 1$$
$$\frac{dx_2}{dt} = x_1 - 2x_2 - 3, x_2(0) = 1.$$

3.8   Solve
$$\frac{dx_1}{dt} = x_2 + 2 - e^{-t}, \ x_1(0) = 1$$
$$\frac{dx_2}{dt} = -x_1 + 1, x_2(0) = 0.$$

CHAPTER

Laplace Transforms

A third method for solving an initial value problem for a system of ordinary differential equations is by using Laplace transforms. Taking the Laplace transform of a single problem converted the differential equation into an algebraic equation. In the same way, taking the transform of a differential system gives an algebraic system. We solve this system for the transforms of our solutions, in terms of the transform variable, then invert. As with a single equation,

$$L\left(\frac{dx}{dt}\right) = \int_0^\infty \frac{dx}{dt} e^{-pt} dt = x(t)e^{-pt}\Big|_0^\infty - \int_{t=0}^\infty x(t)(-pe^{-pt})dt$$

by integration by parts. Assuming $x(t)$ is exponentially bounded, $\lim_{t\to\infty} x(t)e^{-pt} = 0$ for sufficiently large p. Thus we get

$$L\left(\frac{dx}{dt}\right) = -x(0) + p\int_0^\infty x(t)e^{-pt} dt = pX(p) - x(0)$$

As an example, consider the system:

$$\frac{dx}{dt} + \frac{dy}{dt} + x - 3t = 0$$

$$\frac{dx}{dt} - y - 2t + 1 = 0$$

$$x(0) = 1, \, y(0) = 2 \tag{4.1}$$

We multiply both sides of each equation by e^{-pt}, then integrate with respect to t from 0 to ∞. Defining, $X(p)$ and $Y(p)$ to be the transforms of x and y we get:

$$\int_0^\infty \frac{dx}{dt} e^{-pt}dt + \int_0^\infty \frac{dy}{dt} e^{-pt}dt + X(p) - \frac{3}{p^2} = 0$$

$$\int_0^\infty \frac{dx}{dt} e^{-pt}dt - Y(p) - \frac{2}{p^2} + \frac{1}{p} = 0, \tag{4.2}$$

which gives us (bearing in mind that $x(0)$ and $y(0)$ are given) the system

$$p X(p) - 1 + p Y(p) - 2 + X(p) - \frac{3}{p^2} = 0$$

$$p X(p) - 1 - Y(p) - \frac{2}{p^2} + \frac{1}{p} = 0.$$

This can be written as

$$\begin{pmatrix} p+1 & p \\ p & -1 \end{pmatrix} \begin{pmatrix} X \\ Y \end{pmatrix} = \begin{pmatrix} 3 + \dfrac{3}{p^2} \\ 1 - \dfrac{1}{p} + \dfrac{2}{p^2} \end{pmatrix}. \tag{4.3}$$

Using Gaussian elimination (or whatever is your favorite method for solving linear systems) we find that

$$X = \frac{p^3 + 2p^2 + 2p + 3}{p^2(p^2 + p + 1)}$$

$$Y = \frac{2p^3 + 2p - 2}{p^2(p^2 + p + 1)}$$

Partial fraction decomposition yields:

$$X(p) = \frac{-1}{p} + \frac{3}{p^2} + \frac{2p}{p^2 + p + 1} = \frac{-1}{p} + \frac{3}{p^2} + \frac{2\left(p + \dfrac{1}{2}\right) - 1}{\left(p + \dfrac{1}{2}\right)^2 + \left(\dfrac{\sqrt{3}}{2}\right)^2}$$

$$X(p) = \frac{4}{p} + \frac{-2}{p^2} + \frac{2p - 2}{p^2 + p + 1} = \frac{4}{p} + \frac{-2}{p^2} + \frac{-2\left(p + \dfrac{1}{2}\right) - 1}{\left(p + \dfrac{1}{2}\right)^2 + \left(\dfrac{\sqrt{3}}{2}\right)^2}. \tag{4.4}$$

Thus inverting the transform gives

$$x(t) = -1 + 3t + 2e^{\frac{-t}{2}} \cos\frac{\sqrt{3}}{2}t - \frac{2\sqrt{3}}{3}e^{\frac{-t}{2}} \sin\frac{\sqrt{3}}{2}t$$

$$y(t) = 4 - 2t - 2e^{\frac{-t}{2}} \cos\frac{\sqrt{3}}{2}t - \frac{2\sqrt{3}}{3}e^{\frac{-t}{2}} \sin\frac{\sqrt{3}}{2}t. \tag{4.5}$$

One of the important uses for the Laplace transform technique is in solving differential equations with discontinuous forcing. To see this let us first look at the transform of a function shifted on the t axis. The Laplace transform of a function, $f(t)$, is defined as $F(p) = \int_0^\infty e^{-pt} f(t)dt$.

This clearly depends only on the values of f for positive values of t. If we want to shift f to the right by a, whatever is between 0 and a will not have affected the transform before. So that it still won't, set the shifted f to be zero up to a (see Figure 4.I).

Of course, if we take some particular function and shift it, the result will not necessarily be zero from 0 to a, therefore we force it to be, by multiplying by

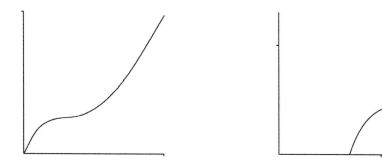

Figure 4.1

$H(t-a)$. $H(t)$, the Heaviside function, is zero for negative arguments, one for positive. Now consider the transform of H(t-a) f(t-a):

$$L(H(t-a)f(t-a)) = \int_0^\infty e^{-pt} H(t-a) f(t-a)dt = \int_a^\infty e^{-pt} f(t-a)dt =$$

$$\int_0^\infty e^{-p(s+a)} f(s)ds = e^{-pa} \int_0^\infty e^{-ps} f(s)ds = e^{-pa} L(f) = e^{-pa} F(p).$$

Thus we get

$$L(H(t-a)\ f(t-a)) = e^{-pa} L\ (f(t)) \tag{4.6}$$

or, in a form that will be easier to use at times,

$$L\,(H(t-a)\,g(t)) = e^{-pa}\,L\,(g(t+a)).\tag{4.7}$$

Many functions with jump discontinuities in the function or in the derivative of some order, or functions with piecewise definitions, can be written in terms of Heaviside functions. The function $H(t-a)$ acts as a switch, turning on at time a. For instance, consider the function in Figure 4.2.

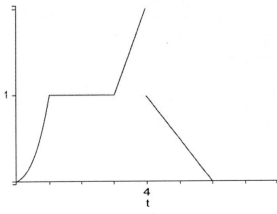

Figure 4.2

The function is given by

$$f(t) = \begin{cases} t^2 & ;0<t<1 \\ 1 & ;t<t<3 \\ t-2 & ;3<t<4 \\ 3-\dfrac{1}{2}t & ;4<t<6 \\ 0 & ;t>6. \end{cases}$$

so there are changes at 1, 3, 4 and 6. We write $f(t)=[\ ]+H(t-1)[\ ]+H(t-3)[\ ]+H(t-4)[\ ]+H(t-6)[\ ]$. For $t<1$ only the first piece is "on", so it must be t^2; for t between I and 3, the first two pieces are on, so they must total to 1. The first is t^2, so the second is $1-t^2$. Similarly, the first three must add to $t-2$, the first two give 1, so the third is $t-3$; $t-2$ plus the fourth is $3-\dfrac{1}{2}t$, so the fourth is $5-\dfrac{3}{2}t$; $3--\dfrac{1}{2}t$ plus the fifth is 0, the fifth must be $\dfrac{1}{2}t-3$. Thus we obtain

$$f(t) = t^2 + H(t-1)[1-t^2] + H(t-3)[t-3] + H(t-4)\left[5 - \frac{3}{2}t\right] + H(t-6)\left[\frac{1}{2}t - 3\right].$$

As an example of how this works on a differential equation, consider the system

$$\frac{dx}{dt} = x + 2y \qquad x(0) = 1$$

$$\frac{dy}{dt} = -3x - 4y + r(t) \qquad y(0) = 0 \tag{4.8}$$

where $r(t)$ is given in Figure 4.3.

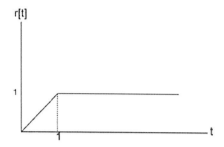

Figure 4.3

Laplace transforms give

$$pX(p) - 1 = X + 2Y$$

$$pY(p) = -3X - 4Y + \mathsf{L}\,(r(t))$$

or

$$(p-1)X - 2Y = 1$$

$$3X + (p+4)Y = R(p) \tag{4.9}$$

We see from Figure 3.3 that $r(t) = t + H\,(t-1)(1-t)$, so

$$R(p) = \mathsf{L}(t + H(t-1)(1-t)) = \mathsf{L}(t) + \mathsf{L}(H(t-1)[1-t])$$

$$(\text{by } 4.7) = \frac{1}{p^2} + e^{-p}\,\mathsf{L}(1-(t+1)) = \frac{1}{p^2} + e^{-p}\mathsf{L}(-t) = \frac{1-e^{-p}}{p^2}$$

Thus

$$\begin{pmatrix} p-1 & -2 \\ 3 & P+4 \end{pmatrix} \begin{pmatrix} X \\ Y \end{pmatrix} = \begin{pmatrix} 1 \\ \dfrac{1-e^{-p}}{p^2} \end{pmatrix} \tag{4.10}$$

Solving by Gaussian elimination yields, after some arithmetic

$$X(p) = \frac{(p^3 + 4p^2 + 2) - 2e^p}{p^2(p+1)(p+2)}$$

$$Y(p) = \frac{(-3p^2 + p - 1) + (-p + 1)e^p}{p^2(p+1)(p+2)}. \tag{4.11}$$

Now we must do partial fraction decomposition separately for the parts multiplied by e^{-p} and those parts not. Partial fractions give

$$\frac{p^3 + 4p^2 + 2}{p^2(p+1)(p+2)} = \frac{-\frac{3}{2}}{p} + \frac{1}{p^2} + \frac{5}{p+1} + \frac{-\frac{5}{2}}{p+2}$$

$$\frac{-2}{p^2(p+1)(p+2)} = \frac{\frac{3}{2}}{p} + \frac{-1}{p^2} + \frac{-2}{p+1} + \frac{\frac{1}{2}}{p+2}$$

$$\frac{-3p^2 + p - 1}{p^2(p+1)(p+2)} = \frac{\frac{5}{4}}{p} + \frac{-\frac{1}{2}}{p^2} + \frac{-5}{p+1} + \frac{+\frac{15}{4}}{p+2}$$

$$\frac{-p + 1}{p^2(p+1)(p+2)} = \frac{-\frac{5}{4}}{p} + \frac{\frac{1}{2}}{p^2} + \frac{2}{p+1} + \frac{-\frac{3}{4}}{p+2} \tag{4.12}$$

Thus we have

$$X(p) = \frac{-\frac{3}{2}}{p} + \frac{1}{p^2} + \frac{5}{p+1} + \frac{-\frac{5}{2}}{p+2} + e^{-p}\left(\frac{\frac{3}{2}}{p} - \frac{1}{p^2} - \frac{2}{p+1} + \frac{\frac{1}{2}}{p+2}\right)$$

$$= \mathsf{L}\left(\frac{-3}{2} + t + 5e^{-t} - \frac{5}{2}e^{-2t}\right) + e^{-p}\mathsf{L}\left(\frac{3}{2} - t - 2e^{-t} + \frac{1}{2}e^{-2t}\right)$$

$$Y(p) = \frac{\frac{5}{4}}{p} + \frac{-\frac{1}{2}}{p^2} + \frac{-5}{p+1} + \frac{\frac{15}{4}}{p+2} + e^{-p}\left(\frac{-\frac{5}{4}}{p} + \frac{\frac{1}{2}}{p^2} + \frac{2}{p+1} + \frac{-\frac{3}{4}}{p+2}\right)$$

$$= \mathsf{L}\left(\frac{5}{4} - \frac{1}{2}t - 5e^{-t} + \frac{15}{4}e^{-2t}\right) + e^{-p}\mathsf{L}\left(\frac{-5}{4} + \frac{1}{2}t + 2e^{-t} - \frac{3}{4}e^{-2t}\right)$$

Finally, using (3.6), we find the solution:

$$x(t) = \frac{-3}{2} + t + 5e^{-t} - \frac{5}{2}e^{-2t}$$

$$+ H(t-1)\left[\frac{3}{2} - (t-1) - 2e^{-(t-1)} + \frac{1}{2}e^{-2(t-1)}\right]$$

$$y(t) = \frac{-5}{4} - \frac{1}{2}t - 5e^{-t} + \frac{15}{4}e^{-2t}$$

$$+ H(t-1)\left[\frac{5}{4} + \frac{1}{2}(t-1) + 2e^{-(t-1)} - \frac{3}{4}e^{-2(t-1)}\right]. \tag{4.14}$$

This may seem outrageously long and complicated, but it is vastly easier than solving the initial value problem with $r(t) = t$ on the interval $[0,1]$, then solving another initial value problem with $r(t) = 1$ on the interval $[1,\infty)$ with initial conditions given by requiring $x(t)$ and $y(t)$ to be continuous with the previous solution at $t = 1$. Further, for an example like this one, where r is continuous but r' is not, $\frac{dx}{dt}$ and $\frac{dy}{dt}$ should actually be continuous; the Laplace transform technique does this automatically.

(For comparison, see problem #4.4.)

EXERCISES

4.1   Use Laplace transform techniques to solve exercises 2.3, 2.4 and 2.5.

4.2   Use Laplace transforms to solve exercises 3.7 and 3.8.

4.3   Solve

$$2\frac{dx}{dt} - \frac{dy}{dt} + x + y = e^{-t}$$

$$\frac{dx}{dt} + \frac{dy}{dt} - 2x = t^2$$

$$x(0) = 0, \ y(0) = 3$$

4.4   Referring to figure 4.4; solve

$$\frac{dx}{dt} + 4x - 3y = r(t) \quad x(0) = 1$$

$$\frac{dy}{dt} + 2x - y = 0 \qquad y(0) = 0$$

two ways:

(a) by solving the problem separately on the two intervals and requiring x and y to be continuous (Why?)

(b) Using Laplace Transforms.

(c) Do your answers agree?

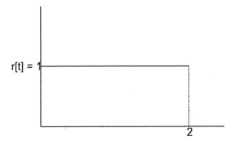

Figure 4.4:

4.5 Referring to Figure 4.5; solve $\dfrac{d}{dt}x = \begin{pmatrix} -2 & -1 \\ 1 & 0 \end{pmatrix} x + \begin{pmatrix} r(t) \\ 0 \end{pmatrix}, x(0) = 0$

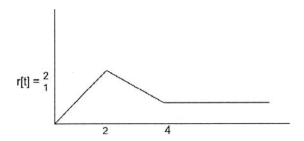

Figure 4.5:

Electric Circuits

One place where systems of differential equations arise is in the study of electric circuits. If a resistor has an electric current flowing through it, there is a difference in the electric potential, or a voltage drop, between the two ends of the resistor. This voltage drop is proportional to the current, so

$$E_R = RI(t) \tag{5.1}$$

where R is the resistance, a property of a particular resistor, given in ohms and normally constant; I is the current in amperes, a function of time; and the voltage drop E_R is measured in volts. This equation is known as Ohm's law. Other empirical formulas for the voltage drops due to common circuit elements are also known. The voltage drop for an inductor is proportional not to the current, but to the time rate of change of the current:

$$E_L = L\frac{dI(t)}{dt}. \tag{5.2}$$

The inductance L is measured in henrys and is a constant of a particular inductor; time is measured in seconds. In a capacitor, the voltage drop is proportional to the charge on the capacitor:

$$E_C = \frac{1}{C}\, Q(t) \tag{5.3}$$

where C, the capacitance, is measured in farads and the charge Q in coulombs. The charge is related to the current by

$$\frac{dQ(t)}{dt} = I(t). \tag{5.4}$$

There are, of course, many other circuit elements, but their voltage drops are not usually linear transformations of the current, so we are not yet prepared to deal with them. Now if we have a circuit with several of these elements and a voltage source, then the voltage drops are related by Kirchoff's second law which states that the sum of the voltage drops around a closed loop of an electric circuit is equal to the applied voltage. For a circuit with a resistor with resistance R, an inductor (inductance L) a capacitor (capacitance C) and a voltage source $E(t)$ (see Figure 5.1)

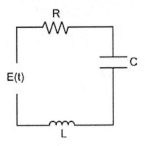

Figure 5.1

we get

$$R\,I(t) + L\frac{dI}{dt} + \frac{l}{C}Q(t) = E(t). \tag{5.5}$$

(From now on we will use R,L,C to refer both to the circuit elements and to the constants associated with them.) This, together with equation (5.4) gives

$$\frac{d}{dt}\begin{pmatrix} Q \\ I \end{pmatrix} = \begin{pmatrix} 0 & 1 \\ \dfrac{-1}{LC} & \dfrac{-R}{L} \end{pmatrix}\begin{pmatrix} Q \\ I \end{pmatrix} + \begin{pmatrix} 0 \\ \dfrac{E(t)}{L} \end{pmatrix}, \tag{5.6}$$

a nonhomogeneous system of two linear differential equations. As an example, consider an RLC circuit with $R=.6$ ohms, $L=.1$ henry, $C=10$ farads and $E(t) = \dfrac{(\sin t)}{10}$ volts. At time $t=0$, take the charge on the capacitor and the current to be zero. This gives

$$\frac{d}{dt}\begin{pmatrix} Q \\ I \end{pmatrix} = \begin{pmatrix} 0 & 1 \\ -1 & -6 \end{pmatrix}\begin{pmatrix} Q \\ I \end{pmatrix} + \begin{pmatrix} 0 \\ \sin t \end{pmatrix},$$

$$\begin{pmatrix} Q(0) \\ I(0) \end{pmatrix} = \begin{pmatrix} 0 \\ 0 \end{pmatrix}. \tag{5.7}$$

The determinant of $A - \lambda I = \lambda^2 + 6\lambda + 1$ so the eigenvalues are $\lambda = -3 \pm \sqrt{8}$. For

$\lambda = -3 + \sqrt{8}$, the eigenvector is $u_i = \begin{pmatrix} -1 \\ 3 - \sqrt{8} \end{pmatrix}$. For the other, $u_2 = \begin{pmatrix} -1 \\ 3 + \sqrt{8} \end{pmatrix}$. We see

that $\dfrac{u_1 - u_2}{-2\sqrt{8}} = \begin{pmatrix} 0 \\ 1 \end{pmatrix}$ so $\begin{pmatrix} 0 \\ E(t) \end{pmatrix} = \dfrac{-E(t)}{2\sqrt{8}} u_1 + \dfrac{E(t)}{2\sqrt{8}} u_2$. Our equation becomes,

$$\frac{d}{dt}\left[a_1(t) \begin{pmatrix} -1 \\ 3 - \sqrt{8} \end{pmatrix} + a_2(t) \begin{pmatrix} -1 \\ 3 + \sqrt{8} \end{pmatrix} \right] =$$

$$\begin{pmatrix} 0 & 1 \\ -1 & -6 \end{pmatrix} \left[a_1(t) \begin{pmatrix} -1 \\ 3 - \sqrt{8} \end{pmatrix} + a_2(t) \begin{pmatrix} -1 \\ 3 + \sqrt{8} \end{pmatrix} \right] +$$

$$\frac{\sin t}{2\sqrt{8}} \left[-\begin{pmatrix} -1 \\ 3 - \sqrt{8} \end{pmatrix} + \begin{pmatrix} -1 \\ 3 = \sqrt{8} \end{pmatrix} \right] \tag{5.8}$$

or

$$\frac{da_1}{dt} u_1 + \frac{da_2}{dt} u_2 = \left(-3 + \sqrt{8}\right) a_1(t) u_1 + \left(-3 - \sqrt{8}\right) a_2(t) u_2 - \frac{\sin t}{2\sqrt{8}} u_1 + \frac{\sin t}{2\sqrt{8}} u_2. \tag{5.9}$$

Our initial conditions translate to $a_1(0) = 0 = a_2(0)$, thus we get

$$\frac{da_1}{dt} = \left(-3 + \sqrt{8}\right) a_1(t) - \frac{\sin t}{2\sqrt{8}}, a_1(0) = 0$$

$$\frac{da_2}{dt} = \left(-3 - \sqrt{8}\right) a_2(t) + \frac{\sin t}{2\sqrt{8}}, a_2(0) = 0. \tag{5.10}$$

These are uncoupled, linear first order equations which we can solve. The solutions are:

$$a_1(t) = \left[\frac{-8 - 3\left(\sqrt{8}\right)}{96}\right] e^{\left(-3 + \sqrt{8}\right)t} - \frac{\sqrt{8}}{96} \sin t + \frac{8 + 3\sqrt{8}}{96} \cos t$$

$$a_2(t) = \left[\frac{3\sqrt{8} - 8}{96}\right] e^{\left(-3 - \sqrt{8}\right)t} + \frac{\sqrt{8}}{96} \sin t + \frac{8 - 3\sqrt{8}}{96} \cos t. \tag{5.11}$$

Thus we get

$$\begin{pmatrix} Q \\ I \end{pmatrix} = a_1(t) \begin{pmatrix} -1 \\ 3 - \sqrt{8} \end{pmatrix} + a_2(t) \begin{pmatrix} -1 \\ 3 + \sqrt{8} \end{pmatrix} \tag{5.12}$$

$$= \begin{pmatrix} \dfrac{\left[\left(8 + 3\sqrt{8}\right) e^{\left(-3+\sqrt{8}\right)t} + \left(8 - 3\sqrt{8}\right) e^{\left(-3-\sqrt{8}\right)t} \right]}{96} - \dfrac{\cos t}{6} \\[4mm] \dfrac{\left[-\sqrt{8} e^{\left(-3+\sqrt{8}\right)t} \right] + \sqrt{8} e^{\left(-3-\sqrt{8}\right)t}}{96} + \dfrac{\sin t}{6} \end{pmatrix}. \tag{5.13}$$

For another example, consider a system with

$R = 2$, $L = 1$, $C = \dfrac{1}{2}$, $E(t) = 12$, $I(0) = 0$ and $Q(0) = 2$. This gives us the system:

$$\frac{d}{dt} \begin{pmatrix} Q \\ I \end{pmatrix} = \begin{pmatrix} 0 & 1 \\ -2 & -2 \end{pmatrix} \begin{pmatrix} Q \\ I \end{pmatrix} + \begin{pmatrix} 0 \\ 12 \end{pmatrix}, \begin{pmatrix} Q(0) \\ I(0) \end{pmatrix} = \begin{pmatrix} 2 \\ 0 \end{pmatrix}.$$

$det(A - \lambda I) = \lambda^2 + 2\lambda + 2$, so $\lambda = -1 \pm i$. For $\lambda_1 = -1 + i, u_1 = \begin{pmatrix} 1 \\ -1+i \end{pmatrix}$;

$\lambda_2 = -1 - i, u_2 = \begin{pmatrix} 1 \\ -1-i \end{pmatrix}$.

We see that

$\begin{pmatrix} 0 \\ 1 \end{pmatrix} = \left(\dfrac{1}{2i} \right)(u_1 - u_2)$ and $\begin{pmatrix} 1 \\ 0 \end{pmatrix} = \dfrac{1-i}{2} u_1 + \dfrac{1+i}{2} u_2$. Letting $\begin{pmatrix} Q \\ I \end{pmatrix} = a_1(t)u_1 + a_2(t)u_2$

gives

$$\frac{da_1}{dt} = \left(-1+i\right) a_1(t) - 6i, \quad a_1(0) = 1 - i$$

$$\frac{da_2}{dt} = \left(-1-i\right) a_2(t) + 6i, \quad a_2(0) = 1 + i. \tag{5.14}$$

The matrix, nonhomogeneity and initial conditions are real; the solution should be real also. Since $\lambda_2 = conj(\lambda_1)$, $u_2 = conj(u_1)$, we will have $a_2(t) = conj[a_1(t)]$. Solving the first equation of (5.14) gives:

$$a_1(t) = \left[1 - i - \left(\frac{6i}{(-1+i)} \right) \right] e^{(-1+i)t} + \frac{6i}{-1+i}$$

or:

$$a_1(t) = [(-2\cos t - 2\sin t) + (2\cos t - 2\sin t)i]e^{-t} + 3 - 3i. \quad (5.15)$$

Thus

$$a_2(t) = [(-2\cos t - 2\sin t) - (2\cos t - 2\sin t)i]e^{-t} + 3 + 3i. \quad (5.16)$$

Substituting (5.15) and (5.16) into our expression for $\begin{pmatrix} Q \\ I \end{pmatrix}$ gives

$$\begin{pmatrix} Q \\ I \end{pmatrix} = \begin{pmatrix} (-4\cos t - 4\sin t)e^{-t} + 6 \\ 8\sin t e^{-t} \end{pmatrix} \quad (5.17)$$

Another applied source of systems of ODEs is a mass-spring system. By Newton's second law, the time derivative of momentum is equal to the sum of the forces. If the mass is constant, we get the mass times acceleration equals force. For a mass on a spring, there are in general three forces: gravity, the spring force and friction.

The force due to the spring is a function of how far the spring is stretched. If the spring is not stretched (or compressed) too far, we can take this force to be a linear function. If x is the length by which the spring has been stretched (negative stretching is compression), then the spring force is given by $-kx$, where k is a positive constant that depends on the spring; k is referred to as the spring constant. The negative sign is because the force is in the opposite direction of the stretching. The force due to friction is normally also taken to be linear, but a linear function of velocity. Thus we have $-c \dfrac{dx}{dt}$ where again c is a positive constant that depends on the system. If there is no other force, we have the equation

$$m \frac{d^2x}{dt^2} = -c \frac{dx}{dt} - kx + mg. \quad (5.18)$$

This system is at rest when $\dfrac{d^2x}{dt^2}$ and $\dfrac{dx}{dt} = 0$, which implies $kx + mg = 0$. This happens at $x = x^* = \dfrac{mg}{k}$. Let us shift our problem to make this the point from which we measure displacement. Define $y = x - \dfrac{mg}{k}$. Substituting this into (5.18) gives

$$m\frac{d^2y}{dt^2} + c\frac{dy}{dt} + ky = 0. \tag{5.19}$$

If there is an external, time dependent forcing in the problem, we have

$$m\frac{d^2y}{dt^2} + c\frac{dy}{dt} + ky = r(t). \tag{5.20}$$

In order to put (5.20) in the form of a system of first order equations, we use $v = \dfrac{dy}{dt}$, and $\dfrac{d^2y}{dt^2} = \dfrac{dv}{dt}$. This gives

$$\frac{dy}{dt} = v$$

$$m\frac{dv}{dt} + cv + ky = r(t) \tag{5.21}$$

or

$$\frac{d}{dt}\begin{pmatrix} y \\ v \end{pmatrix} = \begin{pmatrix} 0 & 1 \\ -\dfrac{k}{m} & -\dfrac{c}{m} \end{pmatrix}\begin{pmatrix} y \\ v \end{pmatrix} + \begin{pmatrix} 0 \\ \dfrac{1}{m}r(t) \end{pmatrix} \tag{5.22}$$

an equation of the same form as (5.6). This equivalence between mechanical and electrical systems is useful for intuition, and is also sometimes used in design. An electric circuit can be designed to mimic a complicated mechanical system. It can be shown that the eigenvalues of a system of the form (5.6) or (5.22) always have negative real parts. If the eigenvalues are distinct, real negative roots, as in our first example, the system is said to be overdamped. If the roots are a complex conjugate pair with negative real part, as in our second example, the system is called underdamped. The third possibility, a double negative root, which is said to be critically damped, will be dealt with in the next section.

EXERCISES

5.1 Verify that (5.11) satisfies (5.10).

5.2 Verify that (5.12) satisfies (5.7).

For Problems 5.3 - 5.5 see Figure 5.2.

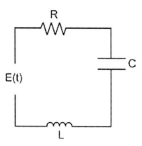

R

C

E(t)

L

Figure 5.2

5.3 Solve the RLC circuit in Figure 5.2 with $R = 5$, $L = 1$, $c = \dfrac{1}{6}$, and $E(t) = \cos t$. Let $Q(0) = 0$, $I(0) = 0$.

5.4 Solve with $R = 4, L = 1, C = \dfrac{1}{5}$ and $E(t) = 6$. Let $Q(0)$ $0, I(0)$ 0.

5.5 Solve with $R = 7, L = 1, C = \dfrac{1}{10}, E(t) = 0$. Let $Q(0) = 5, I(0) = 0$.

5.6 Suppose $x(t) = a_1(t)u_1 + a_2(t)u_2$ and $x(t)$ is real valued. If u_1 and u_2 are linearly independent and $u_2 = conj(u_1)$ show that $a_2(t) = conj[a_1(t)]$. (Hint: take the complex conjugate of both sides and use linear independence.)

5.7 Show that if b, c are real positive numbers, the eigenvalues of $\begin{pmatrix} 0 & 1 \\ -c & -b \end{pmatrix}$ are either both negative reals or complex conjugates with negative real part.

(a) Find the eigenvalues using the quadratic equation.

(b) If the roots are complex, what is their real part?

(c) If the roots are real, why are they both negative? (Recall $c > 0$.)

5.8   Of the important constants for a mass spring system, g is known and m can readily be measured; x^* can also be measured so k can be found. The friction coefficient is a bit trickier to get. Suppose a 100 gram mass stretches a given spring 5 cm at rest. What is k? The spring is stretched an additional 10 cm and released. ($y(0) = ?$ $v(0) = ?$) The mass oscillates. When the mass comes back to the bottom, it is only 9 cm below its at rest position. Solve for c.

Generalized Eigenvectors

Consider an electric circuit with $R = 2, L = \dfrac{1}{3}, C = \dfrac{1}{3}, E(t) = 0, Q(0) = 1, I(0) = 0..$

This gives

$$\frac{d}{dt}\begin{pmatrix} Q \\ I \end{pmatrix} = \begin{pmatrix} 0 & 1 \\ -9 & -6 \end{pmatrix}\begin{pmatrix} Q \\ I \end{pmatrix}, \begin{pmatrix} Q \\ I \end{pmatrix}(0) = \begin{pmatrix} 1 \\ 0 \end{pmatrix} \tag{6.1}$$

If we take the determinant of $A - \lambda I$, and set it equal to zero, we get $\lambda^2 + 6\lambda + 9 = 0$, so $\lambda = -3$ is a double root. To get the eigenvectors, we consider the kernel of $A + 3I$,

$$\begin{pmatrix} 3 & 1 \\ -9 & -3 \end{pmatrix}\begin{pmatrix} x \\ y \end{pmatrix} = \begin{pmatrix} 0 \\ 0 \end{pmatrix} \text{ so } \begin{pmatrix} x \\ y \end{pmatrix} = a\begin{pmatrix} 1 \\ -3 \end{pmatrix} \tag{6.2}$$

for any a. Thus we get only one linearly independent eigenvector. How can we proceed, since one vector is not enough to span $\mathbb{R}^2$? We could, of course, solve (6.1) using the methods from Section 2, but there is another way. Let us consider, in general, a 2 x 2 matrix A, with a double eigenvalue λ, but only one linearly independent eigenvector, which we call u_1. Thus $A\, u_1 = \lambda u_1$, and there is no vector v, not a multiple of u_1, such that $Av = mv$. Let u_2 be any vector in R^2 linearly independent of u_1. Since u_1 and u_2 span R^2, any vector can be written as a linear combination of u_1 and u_2. In particular we can find a, b in R such that

$$Au_2 = au_1 + bu_2. \tag{6.3}$$

We know that a is not 0, since u_1 is the only eigenvector. Now consider

$$A(u_2 - ku_1) = Au_2 - kAu_1 = au_1 - bu_2 - k\lambda u_1$$
$$= [a + k(b - \lambda)]u_1 + b(u_2 - ku_1). \tag{6.4}$$

Again, we know that u_1 is the only eigenvector, so for any value of $k, [a + k(b - \lambda)]$ is not 0. This implies that $b - \lambda = 0$ $\left[\text{otherwise let } k = \dfrac{-a}{b - \lambda}\right]$ Thus we find that for any u_2 linearly independent of u_1, $A\,u_2 = a\,u_1 + \lambda\,u_2$, $a \neq 0$.

By letting $u_2^* = \left(\dfrac{1}{a}\right)u_2$, we see that when u_1 is the only eigenvector, we can always solve (although not uniquely)

$$Au_2^* = u_1 + \lambda u_2^*. \tag{6.5}$$

When u_1 is an eigenvector of A with eigenvalue λ, a solution to (6.5) is called a generalized eigenvector. Let us find a generalized eigenvector for the matrix in system (6.I) and see how it can be used to solve the differential equations. For this matrix $\lambda = -3$ and $u_1 = \begin{pmatrix} 1 \\ -3 \end{pmatrix}$, so we need to solve $Au_2 = u_1 - 3u_2$ or $(a + 3I)u_2 = u_1$.

That is, solve:

$$\begin{pmatrix} 3 & 1 \\ -9 & -3 \end{pmatrix}\begin{pmatrix} x \\ y \end{pmatrix} = \begin{pmatrix} 1 \\ -3 \end{pmatrix}. \tag{6.6}$$

This has the solution $y = 1 - 3x$, thus one solution (which is all we need) is $x = 0, y = 1$. Let $u_2 = \begin{pmatrix} 0 \\ 1 \end{pmatrix}$, Now u_1 and u_2 span $\mathbb{R}^2$, so let

$$\begin{pmatrix} Q \\ I \end{pmatrix} = a_1(t)u_1 + a_2(t)u_2. \tag{6.7}$$

Substituting (6.7) into (6.1) yields

$$\frac{da_1}{dt}u_1 + \frac{da_2}{dt}u_2 = a_1(t)Au_1 + a_2(t)Au_2$$

$$= a_1(t)\lambda u_1 + a_2(t)(u_1 + \lambda u_2) \tag{6.8}$$

so equating coefficients gives

$$\frac{da_1}{dt} = \lambda a_1(t) + a_2(t)$$

$$\frac{da_2}{dt} = \lambda a_2(t).$$

(6.9)

This system is not completely uncoupled, but by starting with the second equation we can solve it. The second equation leads immediately to $a_2(t) = k_2 e^{\lambda t}$. Substituting this into the first gives

$$\frac{da_1}{dt} = \lambda a_1(t) + k_2 e^{\lambda t}.$$

(6.10)

Variation of parameters or the method of undetermined coefficients gives the solution to this: $a_1(t) = k_1 e^{\lambda t} + k_2 t e^{\lambda t}$. Thus we get (since $\lambda = -3$)

$$\begin{pmatrix} Q \\ I \end{pmatrix} = \left(k_1 e^{-3t} + k_2 t e^{-3t} \right) \begin{pmatrix} 1 \\ -3 \end{pmatrix} + k_2 e^{3t} \begin{pmatrix} 0 \\ 1 \end{pmatrix}.$$

(6.11)

Initial conditions give us $\begin{pmatrix} Q(0) \\ I(0) \end{pmatrix} = k_1 \begin{pmatrix} 1 \\ -3 \end{pmatrix} + k_2 \begin{pmatrix} 0 \\ 1 \end{pmatrix} = \begin{pmatrix} 1 \\ 0 \end{pmatrix}$

so $k_1 = 1, k_2 = 3$, and

$$\begin{pmatrix} Q(t) \\ I(t) \end{pmatrix} = \begin{pmatrix} e^{-3t} + 3t e^{-3t} \\ -9t e^{-3t} \end{pmatrix}$$

(6.12)

It is worth noting that the generalized eigenvectors can be used in the same manner that ordinary eigenvectors are used to diagonalize a matrix. Of course a matrix such as the one in system (6.1) can't be diagonalized, since an n x n matrix is diagonalizable if and only if it has n linearly independent eigenvectors. The standard form for matrices that do not have sufficient eigenvectors will turn out to have the eigenvalues down the diagonal (repeated as often as they·were repeated as roots of the characteristic polynomial) some ones in a position directly above the diagonal (on the super-diagonal) and zeroes everywhere else. The number of ones on the super-diagonal is equal to the deficiency of eigenvectors. We will deal more with this later. For now, let us

demonstrate with our matrix $\begin{pmatrix} 0 & 1 \\ -9 & -6 \end{pmatrix}$. The eigenvector is $\begin{pmatrix} 1 \\ -3 \end{pmatrix}$ and the

generalized eigenvector is $\begin{pmatrix} 0 \\ 1 \end{pmatrix}$, so let $P = \begin{pmatrix} 1 & 0 \\ -3 & 1 \end{pmatrix}$. Then $P^{-1} = \begin{pmatrix} 1 & 0 \\ 3 & 1 \end{pmatrix}$, and

$$P^{-1}AP = \begin{pmatrix} 1 & 0 \\ 3 & 1 \end{pmatrix} \begin{pmatrix} 0 & 1 \\ -9 & -6 \end{pmatrix} \begin{pmatrix} 1 & 0 \\ -3 & 1 \end{pmatrix}$$

$$= \begin{pmatrix} 0 & 1 \\ -9 & -3 \end{pmatrix} \begin{pmatrix} 1 & 0 \\ -3 & 1 \end{pmatrix} = \begin{pmatrix} -3 & 1 \\ 0 & -3 \end{pmatrix}. \tag{6.13}$$

This is called the Jordan canonical form for A. The eigenvectors of a matrix should be a smooth function of the entries in the matrix. If we vary the entries of a matrix with a double eigenvalue and only one linearly independent eigenvector, we will (almost always) get a matrix with two eigenvectors. How does the generalized eigenvector relate? For an example, consider the matrix

$$A_\varepsilon = \begin{pmatrix} -4 & -4 \\ 1 - \varepsilon^2 & 0 \end{pmatrix}. \tag{6.14}$$

At $\varepsilon = 0$ we get

$$A_0 = \begin{pmatrix} -4 & -4 \\ 1 & 0 \end{pmatrix} \tag{6.15}$$

A_0 has a double eigenvalue of $\lambda = -2$ with only one linearly independent eigenvector, $u = \begin{pmatrix} -2 \\ 1 \end{pmatrix}$. We can find a generalized eigenvector $v = \begin{pmatrix} 1 \\ 0 \end{pmatrix}$ or anything of the form $\begin{pmatrix} 1 \\ 0 \end{pmatrix} + k \begin{pmatrix} -2 \\ 1 \end{pmatrix}$. If we set the determinant of $A_\varepsilon - \lambda I$ equal to zero, we see that $\lambda = -2 \pm \varepsilon$ and the eigenvectors are:

$$u_1 = \begin{pmatrix} -2 \\ 1 + \dfrac{\varepsilon}{2} \end{pmatrix} \text{ and } u_2 = \begin{pmatrix} -2 \\ 1 - \dfrac{\varepsilon}{2} \end{pmatrix} \tag{6.16}$$

It can readily be seen that as ε approaches 0, both u_1 and u_2 approach the regular eigenvector of $A_0, u_2 = \begin{pmatrix} -2 \\ 1 \end{pmatrix}$. Where do we get the generalized eigenvector? To answer this question, it is easiest to solve an initial value problem. First consider

$$\frac{dx}{dt} = A_0 x, x(0) = \begin{pmatrix} 1 \\ 1 \end{pmatrix}. \tag{6.17}$$

Using u and v as our basis, we write $x = a(t)\begin{pmatrix} -2 \\ 1 \end{pmatrix} + b(t)\begin{pmatrix} 1 \\ 0 \end{pmatrix}$. Substituting this into (6.17) and equating coefficients, we get:

$$\frac{da}{dt} = -2a + b, \; a(0) = 1$$

$$\frac{db}{dt} = -2b, \; b(0) = 3 \tag{6.18}$$

Thus $b = 3e^{-2t}$ so $\frac{da}{dt} + 2a = 3e^{-2t}$ and we get our solution:

$$a = e^{-2t} + 3te^{-2t}$$
$$b = 3e^{-2t} \tag{6.19}$$

or

$$x\left(e^{-2t} + 3te^{-2t}\right)\begin{pmatrix} -2 \\ 1 \end{pmatrix} + 3e^{-2t}\begin{pmatrix} 1 \\ 0 \end{pmatrix}. \tag{6.20}$$

Now consider

$$\frac{dx}{dt} = A_\varepsilon x, x(0) = \begin{pmatrix} 1 \\ 1 \end{pmatrix}, \varepsilon > 0. \tag{6.21}$$

Using our eigenvectors, we write $x = a(t)\begin{pmatrix} -2 \\ 1 + \dfrac{\varepsilon}{2} \end{pmatrix} + b(t)\begin{pmatrix} -2 \\ 1 - \dfrac{\varepsilon}{2} \end{pmatrix}$, giving:

$$\frac{da}{dt} = (-2 + \varepsilon)a$$

$$\frac{db}{dt} = (-2 - \varepsilon)b \tag{6.22}$$

Initial conditions tell us that $a(0)\begin{pmatrix} -2 \\ 1+\dfrac{\varepsilon}{2} \end{pmatrix} + b(0)\begin{pmatrix} -2 \\ 1-\dfrac{\varepsilon}{2} \end{pmatrix} = \begin{pmatrix} 1 \\ 1 \end{pmatrix}$ so (after some algebra):

$$a(0) = \frac{3}{2\varepsilon} - \frac{1}{4}, \quad b(0) = -\frac{3}{2\varepsilon} - \frac{1}{4} \tag{6.23}$$

and our solution is:

$$\mathbf{x}_\varepsilon = \left(\frac{3}{2\varepsilon} - \frac{1}{4} \right) e^{(-2+\varepsilon)t} \begin{pmatrix} -2 \\ 1+\dfrac{\varepsilon}{2} \end{pmatrix} + \left(-\frac{3}{2\varepsilon} - \frac{1}{4} \right) e^{(-2-\varepsilon)t} \begin{pmatrix} -2 \\ 1-\dfrac{\varepsilon}{2} \end{pmatrix} \tag{6.24}$$

What is the limit of (6.24) as $\varepsilon \to 0$? We split (6.24) into 3 pieces:

$$-\frac{1}{4} e^{(-2+\varepsilon)t} \begin{pmatrix} -2 \\ 1+\dfrac{\varepsilon}{2} \end{pmatrix} + \left(-\frac{1}{4} \right) e^{(-2-\varepsilon)t} \begin{pmatrix} -2 \\ 1-\dfrac{\varepsilon}{2} \end{pmatrix} \tag{6.25}$$

$$\frac{3}{2\varepsilon} e^{(-2+\varepsilon)t} \begin{pmatrix} 0 \\ \dfrac{\varepsilon}{2} \end{pmatrix} - \frac{3}{2\varepsilon} e^{(-2-\varepsilon)t} \begin{pmatrix} 0 \\ -\dfrac{\varepsilon}{2} \end{pmatrix} \tag{6.26}$$

and

$$\frac{3}{2\varepsilon} e^{(-2+\varepsilon)t} \begin{pmatrix} -2 \\ 1 \end{pmatrix} - \frac{3}{2\varepsilon} e^{(-2-\varepsilon)t} \begin{pmatrix} -2 \\ 1 \end{pmatrix} \tag{6.27}$$

In a straightforward manner, (6.25) gives

$$-\frac{1}{2} e^{-2t} \begin{pmatrix} -2 \\ 1 \end{pmatrix} \tag{6.28}$$

and (6.26) gives

$$3e^{-2t} \begin{pmatrix} 0 \\ 1 \\ \dfrac{1}{2} \end{pmatrix}. \tag{6.29}$$

(6.27) requires a bit more thought. Factoring off what we can, we have

$$\lim_{\varepsilon \to 0} \frac{3}{2} e^{-2t} \frac{e^{\varepsilon t} - e^{-\varepsilon t}}{\varepsilon} \begin{pmatrix} -2 \\ 1 \end{pmatrix},$$

or

$$\frac{3}{2}e^{-2t}\left[\lim_{\varepsilon\to0}\frac{e^{\varepsilon t}-e^{-\varepsilon t}}{\varepsilon}\right]\binom{-2}{1}.$$

Using L'Hôpital's rule we get

$$\frac{3}{2}e^{-2t}\bullet2t\binom{-2}{1}=3te^{-2t}\binom{-2}{1}. \tag{6.30}$$

Combining (6.28), (6.29) and (6.30) yields:

$$\lim_{\varepsilon\to0}x_\varepsilon(t)=\frac{-1}{2}e^{-2t}\binom{-2}{1}+3e^{-2t}\begin{pmatrix}0\\1\\2\end{pmatrix}+3te^{-2t}\binom{-2}{1}, \tag{6.31}$$

which is the same as our previous solution to (6.17) given in (6.20). The different form is due to the lack of uniqueness of the generalized eigenvector. We used $v=\binom{1}{0}$ but we could just as well have used $\begin{pmatrix}0\\1\\2\end{pmatrix}$.

EXERCISES

6.1 Solve $\dfrac{d}{dt}\binom{Q}{I}=\begin{pmatrix}0&1\\-4&-4\end{pmatrix}\binom{Q}{I}, \binom{Q}{I}(0)=\binom{2}{1}.$

6.2 Solve $\dfrac{d}{dt}\binom{Q}{I}=\begin{pmatrix}0&1\\-16&-8\end{pmatrix}\binom{Q}{I}+\binom{0}{\sin t}, \binom{Q}{I}(0)=\binom{0}{0}.$

6.3 Solve $\dfrac{d}{dt}\binom{x}{y}=\begin{pmatrix}2&1\\-1&4\end{pmatrix}\binom{x}{y}+\binom{2}{3}, \binom{x}{y}(0)=\binom{1}{1}.$

6.4 Find P, P^{-1} to put each of the matrices in Exercises 6.1-6.3 in Jordan canonical form.

6.5 If $A=\begin{pmatrix}3&1\\2&2\end{pmatrix}$ then $L=4, u_1=\binom{1}{1}$ is an eigenvalue-eigenvector pair.

There is no solution to $Au_2=u_1+Lu_2$

(a) Show $\begin{pmatrix} 3 & 1 \\ 2 & 2 \end{pmatrix}\begin{pmatrix} x \\ y \end{pmatrix} = \begin{pmatrix} 1 \\ 1 \end{pmatrix} + 4\begin{pmatrix} x \\ y \end{pmatrix}$ has no solution.

(b) Why doesn't the proof that equation (6.5) is solvable work for this case?

6.6 Show that if A is a 2 x 2 matrix with a double real root of λ, then either $A = \lambda I$, or A is not diagonalizable. (Hint: suppose A is diagonalizable.)

6.7 Consider the matrix $A_\varepsilon = \begin{pmatrix} -4 & -4 \\ 1+\varepsilon^2 & 0 \end{pmatrix}$.

Solve (using eigenvector methods):

$$\frac{dx}{dt} = A_\varepsilon x, x(0) = \begin{pmatrix} 1 \\ 1 \end{pmatrix} \text{ and let } \varepsilon \to 0.$$

CHAPTER

Solution Operators

There is still another way we can solve a system of differential equations of the form (4.1). If we look at the initial value problem in matrix form $\frac{dx}{dt} = Ax;\ x(0) = x_0$, it looks like equation (0.1): $\frac{dx}{dt} = ax;\ x(0) = x_0$. This was solved by (1.2) $x(t) = x_0 e^{at}$. Can we write $x(t) = x_0 e^{at}$? If so, what does e^{At} mean when A is a matrix? Again, consider the scalar case. For a, a real number,

$$e^{at} = \lim_{n \to \infty} \sum_{j=0}^{n} a^j \frac{t^j}{j!}. \tag{7.1}$$

If A is a square matrix, then A^j makes sense for $j \geq 0 \left(A^0 = I \right)$, so we can define the partial sum $\sum_{j=0}^{n} A^j \frac{t^j}{j!}$. Therefore, for A, a square matrix, we define

$$e^{At} = \lim_{n \to \infty} \sum_{j=0}^{n} A^j \frac{t^j}{j!}.$$

We are left with two questions: 1) When does this sequence of partial sums converge and 2) in what way, if at all, is this matrix related to the solution of (4.1)?

First we consider a diagonal matrix. Let $D = \text{diag}(\lambda_1, \lambda_2) = \begin{bmatrix} \lambda_1 & 0 \\ 0 & \lambda_2 \end{bmatrix}$ Squaring D gives $D^2 = \text{diag}(\lambda_1^2, \lambda_2^2)$, cubing gives $\text{diag}(\lambda_1^3, \lambda_2^3)$ and we see that

$D^j = diag\left(\lambda_1^j, \lambda_2^j\right)$ Therefore $e^{Dt} = \lim\limits_{n \to a} \sum\limits_{j=0}^{n} D^j \dfrac{t^j}{j!} = \lim\limits_{n \to \infty} \sum\limits_{j=0}^{n} diag\left(\lambda_1^j \dfrac{t^j}{j!}, \lambda_2^j \dfrac{t^j}{j!}\right)$.

Since addition of matrices is just addition of corresponding elements, this becomes

$$\lim\limits_{n \to \infty}\left[diag\left[\sum\limits_{j=0}^{n}\lambda_1^j \dfrac{t^j}{j!}, \sum\limits_{j=0}^{n}\lambda_2^j \dfrac{t^j}{j!}\right]\right]$$

Taking the limit inside and using the definition of e^a, we get:

$$\text{if } D = diag(\lambda_1, \lambda_2), e^{Dt} = diag\left(e^{\lambda_1 t}, e^{\lambda_2 t}\right) = \begin{bmatrix} e^{\lambda_1 t} & 0 \\ 0 & e^{\lambda_2 t} \end{bmatrix}. \tag{7.2}$$

If A is not diagonal, but is diagonable, we can use (7.2) after some algebra.

Suppose P is the matrix such that $P^{-1}AP = D = diag\left(\lambda_1, \lambda_2\right)$. Then $A = PDP^{-1}$.

Substituting this into (7.l) gives $e^{At} = \lim\limits_{n \to \infty} \sum\limits_{j=0}^{n} A^j \dfrac{t^j}{j!} = \lim\limits_{n \to 0} \sum\limits_{j=0}^{n} \left(PDP^{-1}\right)^j \dfrac{t^j}{j!}$. However,

$$\left(PDP^{-1}\right)^2 = \left(PDP^{-1}\right)\left(PDP^{-1}\right) = PDDP^{-1} = PD^2 P^{-1}.$$

Similarly, $\left(PDP^{-1}\right)^j = PD^j P^{-1}$. Thus $\sum\limits_{j=0}^{n}\left(PDP^{-1}\right)^j \dfrac{t^j}{j!} = \sum\limits_{j=0}^{n} PD^j P^{-1} \dfrac{t^j}{j!} = P\left[\sum\limits_{j=0}^{n} D^j \dfrac{t^j}{j!}\right]P^{-1}$

Taking limits, we get that

$$\text{If } P^{-1}AP = diag(\lambda_1, \lambda_2), e^{At} = P\begin{bmatrix} e^{\lambda_1 t} & 0 \\ 0 & e^{\lambda_2 t} \end{bmatrix}P^{-1}. \tag{7.3}$$

For diagonable matrices, at any rate, e^{At} converges for all t. How is this 2 x 2 matrix related to the solution of (4.l)? Since A is a constant matrix, so is A^j for all

j. Thus $\dfrac{d}{dt}(e^{At}) = \dfrac{d}{dt}\left(\lim\limits_{n \to \infty} \sum\limits_{j=1}^{n} A^j \dfrac{t^j}{j!}\right) = \lim\limits_{n \to \infty}\left(\sum\limits_{j=0}^{n} A^j \dfrac{d}{dt}\left(\dfrac{t^j}{j!}\right)\right) = \lim\limits_{n \to \infty}\left(\sum\limits_{j=0}^{n} A^j \dfrac{t^{j-1}}{(j-1)!}\right)$

$$= \lim\limits_{n \to \infty}\left(\sum\limits_{k=0}^{n} A^{k+1} \dfrac{t^k}{k\lambda}\right) = A\lim\limits_{n \to \infty}\left(\sum\limits_{k=0}^{n} A^k \dfrac{t^k}{k!}\right) = Ae^{At}. \tag{7.4}$$

This will, of course, be true if we multiply e^{At} by any constant. At $t = 0$, $e^{At} = I$ (the first term in the sum that gives us e^{At} is I; all the other terms are multiplied by $t^j, j > 0$). Thus, $x(t) = e^{At}x_0$ gives a vector such that $\dfrac{dx}{dt} = \dfrac{d}{dt}\left(e^{At}x_0\right) = Ae^{At}x_0 = Ax(t)$ and $x(0) = e^{A0}x_0 = Ix_0$, so $x(t) = e^{At}x_0$ is a solution to (4.1).

As an example, let us consider

$$\frac{d}{dt}\begin{bmatrix} x \\ y \end{bmatrix} = \begin{bmatrix} -3 & 3 \\ -1 & 0 \end{bmatrix}\begin{bmatrix} x \\ y \end{bmatrix}, \begin{bmatrix} x \\ y \end{bmatrix}(0) = \begin{bmatrix} 2 \\ 3 \end{bmatrix}. \tag{7.5}$$

The eigenvalues of A are -1 and -2. For $\lambda = -1$, the kernel of $A - \lambda I$ is spanned by $\begin{bmatrix} 1 \\ 1 \end{bmatrix}$, for $\lambda = -2$ by $\begin{bmatrix} 2 \\ 1 \end{bmatrix}$.

$$\text{Let } P = \begin{bmatrix} 1 & 2 \\ 1 & 1 \end{bmatrix}, P^{-1} = \begin{bmatrix} -1 & 2 \\ 1 & -1 \end{bmatrix}, P^{-1}AP = \begin{bmatrix} -1 & 0 \\ 0 & -2 \end{bmatrix}, \text{ so}$$

$$e^{At} = P\begin{bmatrix} e^{-t} & 0 \\ 0 & e^{-2t} \end{bmatrix}P^{-1}$$

$$= \begin{bmatrix} 1 & 2 \\ 1 & 1 \end{bmatrix}\begin{bmatrix} e^{-t} & 0 \\ 0 & e^{-2t} \end{bmatrix}\begin{bmatrix} -1 & 2 \\ 1 & -1 \end{bmatrix}$$

$$= \begin{bmatrix} -e^{-t} + 2e^{-2t} & 2e^{-t} - 2e^{-2t} \\ -e^{-t} + e^{-2t} & 2e^{-t} - e^{-2t} \end{bmatrix}$$

Letting $x(t) = e^{At}x_0$ we get:

$$x(t) = \begin{bmatrix} -e^{-t} + 2e^{-2t} & 2e^{-t} - 2e^{-2t} \\ -e^{-t} + e^{-2t} & 2e^{-t} - e^{-2t} \end{bmatrix}\begin{bmatrix} 2 \\ 3 \end{bmatrix} = \begin{bmatrix} 4e^{-t} - 2e^{-2t} \\ 4e^{-t} - e^{-2t} \end{bmatrix}, \tag{7.6}$$

which is indeed the solution to (7.5).

This also works for complex eigenvalues. Consider the system

$$\frac{dx}{dt} = \begin{bmatrix} 1 & 1 \\ -1 & 1 \end{bmatrix}x, x(0) = \begin{bmatrix} -1 \\ 3 \end{bmatrix}. \tag{7.7}$$

The eigenvalues of the matrix are $1 \pm i$. For $1 + i$, the eigenvector is $\begin{bmatrix} 1 \\ i \end{bmatrix}$; for the

other, $\begin{bmatrix} 1 \\ i \end{bmatrix}$. Thus we get $P = \begin{bmatrix} 1 & 1 \\ i & i \end{bmatrix}$ and $P^{-1} = \begin{bmatrix} \dfrac{1}{2} & -\dfrac{i}{2} \\ \dfrac{1}{2} & \dfrac{i}{2} \end{bmatrix}$. Now

$P^{-1}AP = \begin{bmatrix} 1+i & 0 \\ 0 & 1-i \end{bmatrix}$, so e^{At} is given by

$$e^{At} = P \begin{bmatrix} e^{(1+i)t} & 0 \\ 0 & e^{(1+i)t} \end{bmatrix} P^{-1} = P \begin{bmatrix} e^t(\cos i + i \sin t) & 0 \\ 0 & e^t(\cos i - i \sin t) \end{bmatrix} P^{-1}$$

$$= \begin{bmatrix} e^t \cos t & e^t \sin t \\ -e^t \sin t & e^t \cos t \end{bmatrix}.$$

Thus we get a solution to (7.7):

$$x(t) = e^{At} x_0 = \begin{bmatrix} e^t \cos t & e^t \sin t \\ -e^t \sin t & e^t \cos t \end{bmatrix} \begin{bmatrix} -1 \\ 3 \end{bmatrix} = \begin{bmatrix} -e^t \cos t + 3e^t \sin t \\ e^t \sin t + 3e^t \cos t \end{bmatrix} \qquad (7.8)$$

To see what to do in the case of a nondiagonable matrix, we first need the following:

$$e^{A+B} = e^A e^B \text{ if } AB = BA. \qquad (7.9)$$

(The proof will be left as an exercise.)

Now consider a matrix that cannot be diagonalized. By using generalized eigenvectors, we can find a matrix P that puts A in Jordan canonical form, that is

$$P^{-1}AP = J \qquad (7.10)$$

where J has the eigenvalues (with multiplicity) down the diagonal, some ones and possibly some zeroes on the super-diagonal, and zeroes everywhere else. Thus, for the 2x2 case in particular, J can be written:

$$J = D + S, D = diag(\lambda, \lambda), S = \begin{bmatrix} 0 & 1 \\ 0 & 0 \end{bmatrix}. \qquad (7.11)$$

Now $P^{-1}AP = D + S$, so $A = P(D+S)P^{-1}$ and, since $DS = SD$,

$$e^{At} = Pe^{(D+S)t}P^{-1} = Pe^{Dt}e^{St}P^{-1}. \qquad (7.12)$$

As before, $e^{Dt} = diag(e^{\lambda t}, e^{\lambda t})$. The other piece, e^{St}, we compute directly from the definition. Since $S = \begin{bmatrix} 0 & 1 \\ 0 & 0 \end{bmatrix}, S^2 = \begin{bmatrix} 0 & 0 \\ 0 & 0 \end{bmatrix}$, and all higher powers will also be zero. Thus we get

$$e^{St} = \sum_{j=0}^{n} S^j \frac{t^j}{j!} = I + St = \begin{bmatrix} 1 & t \\ 0 & 1 \end{bmatrix}, \qquad (7.13)$$

and

$$e^{At} = P\left(e^{\lambda t}I\right)\begin{bmatrix} 1 & t \\ 0 & 1 \end{bmatrix}P^{-1} \tag{7.14}$$

As an example, we will solve the system

$$\frac{dx}{dt}\begin{bmatrix} 0 & 1 \\ -4 & -4 \end{bmatrix}x, x(0) = \begin{bmatrix} 3 \\ -2 \end{bmatrix}. \tag{7.15}$$

The matrix A has a double eigenvalue of -2; the kernel of $A + 2I$ is spanned by $\begin{bmatrix} -1 \\ 2 \end{bmatrix}$. Thus the eigenvectors of A do not span $\mathbb{R}^2$, so we look for a generalized eigenvector: solve

$$(A + 2I)\,\mathbf{x} = \begin{bmatrix} -1 \\ 2 \end{bmatrix}. \tag{7.16}$$

We get $y = t, x = \dfrac{-1 - t}{2}$, so let $t = 1$ and get $\begin{bmatrix} -1 \\ 1 \end{bmatrix}$. Now $P = \begin{bmatrix} -1 & -1 \\ 2 & 1 \end{bmatrix}$, $P^{-1} = \begin{bmatrix} 1 & 1 \\ -2 & -1 \end{bmatrix}$ and we get $P^{-1}AP = \begin{bmatrix} -2 & 1 \\ 0 & -2 \end{bmatrix}$. Now, using (7.14)

$$e^{At} = P\begin{bmatrix} e^{-2t} & 0 \\ 0 & e^{-2t} \end{bmatrix}\begin{bmatrix} 1 & t \\ 0 & 1 \end{bmatrix}P^{-1}$$

$$= P\begin{bmatrix} e^{-2t} & te^{-2t} \\ 0 & e^{-2t} \end{bmatrix}P^{-1} \tag{7.17}$$

$$= \begin{bmatrix} e^{-2t} + 2te^{-2t} & te^{-2t} \\ -4te^{-2t} & e^{-2t} - 2te^{-2t} \end{bmatrix}$$

so we get a solution to (7.15):

$$x(t) = e^{At}x_0 = e^{At}\begin{bmatrix} 3 \\ -2 \end{bmatrix} = \begin{bmatrix} 3e^{-2t} + 4te^{-2t} \\ -2e^{-2t} - 8te^{-2t} \end{bmatrix}. \tag{7.18}$$

Equation (7.9) also provides an alternative method of calculating e^{At} when A has complex eigenvalues, that avoids much of the complex arithmetic. To understand this method, we must first review canonical forms.

The earlier methods in this chapter involve using a basis under which A assumes its Jordan canonical form. By using the eigenvectors and generalized eigenvectors as the basis, A becomes a block diagonal matrix, each block being associated with one regular eigenvector and of the form

$$\begin{bmatrix} \lambda & 1 & 0 & \cdots & \cdots & 0 \\ 0 & \lambda & 1 & 0 & \cdots & 0 \\ \vdots & & \ddots & & & \vdots \\ & & & \ddots & & \vdots \\ \vdots & & & & \lambda & 1 \\ 0 & \cdots & \cdots & \cdots & 0 & \lambda \end{bmatrix}$$

(7.19)

(If the block is 1×1, of course, it is just λ.) Any matrix can be put in this form. Another canonical form, the real canonical form, is sometimes more useful when dealing with real matrices that have complex eigenvalues. For this we take as a basis, the real eigenvectors and generalized eigenvectors as before, but each complex conjugate pair of complex eigenvectors or generalized eigenvectors is replaced by their real and imaginary parts. As an example, consider the matrix

$$A = \begin{bmatrix} -3 & 2 \\ -4 & 1 \end{bmatrix}.$$

(7.20)

$Det(A - \lambda I) = \lambda^2 + 2\lambda + 5$, so $\lambda = -1 \pm 2i$. The eigenvector for $\lambda = -1 + 2i$ is

$\begin{bmatrix} 1 \\ 1+i \end{bmatrix}$, so the other eigenvector $\begin{bmatrix} 1 \\ 1-i \end{bmatrix}$. These vectors can be written as $\begin{bmatrix} 1 \\ 1 \end{bmatrix} \pm i \begin{bmatrix} 0 \\ 1 \end{bmatrix}$,

so the real part is $\begin{bmatrix} 1 \\ 1 \end{bmatrix}$ and the imaginary part is $\begin{bmatrix} 0 \\ 1 \end{bmatrix}$. This is what we will use as a

basis. Let $Q = \begin{bmatrix} 1 & 0 \\ 1 & 1 \end{bmatrix}, Q^{-1} = \begin{bmatrix} 1 & 0 \\ -1 & 1 \end{bmatrix}$, then

$$Q^{-1}AQ = Q = \begin{bmatrix} 1 & 0 \\ -1 & 1 \end{bmatrix}\begin{bmatrix} -3 & 2 \\ -4 & 1 \end{bmatrix}\begin{bmatrix} 1 & 0 \\ 1 & 1 \end{bmatrix}$$

$$= \begin{bmatrix} -3 & 2 \\ -1 & -1 \end{bmatrix} \begin{bmatrix} 1 & 0 \\ 1 & 1 \end{bmatrix} \tag{7.21}$$

$$= \begin{bmatrix} -1 & 2 \\ -2 & -1 \end{bmatrix}.$$

This is the real canonical form. In general, the real canonical form is a block diagonal with blocks of the form (7.19) for the real eigenvalues, λ, and of the form

$$\begin{bmatrix} \begin{bmatrix} \alpha & \beta \\ -\beta & \alpha \end{bmatrix} & \begin{bmatrix} 1 & 0 \\ 0 & 1 \end{bmatrix} & 0 \cdots & 0 \\ & \begin{bmatrix} \alpha & \beta \\ -\beta & \alpha \end{bmatrix} & & \vdots \\ 0 & & \ddots & 0 \\ 0 & & & \begin{bmatrix} \alpha & \beta \\ -\beta & \alpha \end{bmatrix} \end{bmatrix} \tag{7.22}$$

for the complex eigenvalues. In exercise 7.5 you will prove this for the 2 x 2 case.

How does this help find e^{At}? Suppose A has eigenvalues $\alpha \pm i\beta$. Then find Q, Q^{-1}, $Q^{-1}AQ = \begin{bmatrix} \alpha & \beta \\ -\beta & \alpha \end{bmatrix}$, so $A = Q \begin{bmatrix} \alpha & \beta \\ -\beta & \alpha \end{bmatrix} = A \begin{bmatrix} \alpha I + \begin{bmatrix} 0 & \beta \\ -\beta & 0 \end{bmatrix} \end{bmatrix} Q^{-1}$. Using

(7.9) we see that $e^{At} = Qe^{\alpha It}e^{\begin{bmatrix} 0 & \beta \\ -\beta & 0 \end{bmatrix}t}Q^{-1} = Q(e^{\alpha t}I)e^{\begin{bmatrix} 0 & \beta \\ -\beta & 0 \end{bmatrix}t}Q^{-1} = e^{\alpha t}Qe^{\begin{bmatrix} 0 & \beta \\ -\beta & 0 \end{bmatrix}t}Q^{-1}$. In Exercise 7.9 you will show that

$$e^{\begin{bmatrix} 0 & \beta \\ -\beta & 0 \end{bmatrix}t} = \begin{bmatrix} \cos\beta & \sin\beta t \\ -\sin\beta t & \cos\beta t \end{bmatrix}. \tag{7.23}$$

Thus

$$e^{At} = e^{\alpha t}Q \begin{bmatrix} \cos\beta t & \sin\beta t \\ -\sin\beta t & \cos\beta t \end{bmatrix} Q^{-1}. \tag{7.24}$$

EXERCISES

7.1 This exercise outlines a proof for equation (7.9).

(a) Write out the first four terms in the sums for e^A, e^B and $e^{(A+B)}$. Do the
    multiplication and show that the zeroth, first, second and third order terms match
    for $(e^A e^B)$ and $e^{(A+B)}$.

(b) Find the kth order term of e^A, e^B (hint: the kth order term will be a sum of terms
    of the form a constant times $A^i B^j$ where $i + j = k$. Both i and j
    will be $\le k$).

(c) What is $\dfrac{(A+B)^k}{k!}$? (Hint: binomial expansion.)

7.2 Find the operator e^{At} for $A = \begin{bmatrix} 3 & 1 \\ 1 & 3 \end{bmatrix}$. Use it to solve $\dfrac{dx}{dt} = \begin{bmatrix} 3 & 1 \\ 1 & 3 \end{bmatrix} x, x(0) = \begin{bmatrix} -2 \\ 3 \end{bmatrix}$.

For 7.3 and 7.4, find the solution operator and solve.

7.3 $\dfrac{dx}{dt} = \begin{bmatrix} 0 & 1 \\ -4 & -5 \end{bmatrix} x, x(0) = \begin{bmatrix} 1 \\ 1 \end{bmatrix}$.

7.4 $\dfrac{dx}{dt} = \begin{bmatrix} 4 & 1 \\ -1 & 2 \end{bmatrix} x, x(0) = \begin{bmatrix} 2 \\ -1 \end{bmatrix}$.

7.5 Suppose A is a real 2 x 2 matrix such that $A(\varphi + i\psi) = (\alpha + i\beta)(\varphi + i\psi)$, where
     φ and ψ are real 2- vectors. Using $\{(\varphi, \psi)\}$ as a basis, find the matrix
     corresponding to A. (Hint $A\varphi = ?, A\psi = ?$).

For 7.6 and 7.7, find e^{At} and solve, using both the Jordan canonical form and the real
canonical ways.

7.6 $\dfrac{d}{dt} x = \begin{bmatrix} -5 & 2 \\ -4 & -1 \end{bmatrix} x, x_0 = \begin{bmatrix} 2 \\ -3 \end{bmatrix}$.

7.7 $\dfrac{d}{dt}x = \begin{bmatrix} -3 & 3 \\ -2 & 1 \end{bmatrix}x, x_0 = \begin{bmatrix} 1 \\ -1 \end{bmatrix}.$

7.8 If ϕ and ψ are as in Exercise 7.5 prove $\{(\phi, \psi)\}$ is linearly independent.

7.9 Using the Jordan canonical form, find e^{At} for $A = \begin{bmatrix} 0 & \beta \\ -\beta & 0 \end{bmatrix}.$

CHAPTER

Numerical Methods

Thus far, we have examined methods of obtaining analytic results; we have been getting our solution as some function of t on an interval (sometimes infinite). Frequently this is either not possible, or, the closed form solution is too unwieldy to be of much use. Numerical solutions are then valuable.

There are many ways of solving differential equations numerically, too many for us to attempt to be complete. Solutions can come in different forms. For the methods we consider here, we will be looking for a series of points that are approximately on the solution curve. Connecting these points give us an approximation to the solution. For instance, if we are trying to approximate some function $y(t)$, we will get a set of points

$$\left\{\left(y_j, t_j\right)\right\}_{j=0}^{M} \tag{8.1}$$

and y_j will be our approximation of $y(t_j)$. For systems of n dependent variables of one independent variable we get a set of points in R^{n+1},

$$\left\{\left(y_{1j}, y_{2j}, \cdots, y_{nj}, t_j\right)\right\}_{j=0}^{M} \tag{8.2}$$

where y_{kj} is our approximation for $y_k(t_j)$. Thus in (8.1) or (8.2) we get an approximation to our solution on the interval $\left[t_0, t_M\right]$.

Many methods are commonly used to obtain the points for the approximation. One of the simplest for first order differential initial value problems is the *Tangent,* or *Euler* method.

For this method we need to know $\dfrac{dy}{dt}$ as a function of y and t, and an initial point, say

$$\frac{dy}{dt} = F(y,t), y(a) = y_0. \tag{8.3}$$

Suppose we want the solution on some t interval $[a,b]$. We partition $[a,b]$ into m pieces (often of equal length) with $a = t_0 < t_1 < t_2 < \cdots < t_m = b$. We assume that each subinterval $[t_j, t_{j+1}]$ is small enough that $\frac{dy}{dt}$ can be treated as a constant on the interval, and take the slope at the left endpoint as our approximation to this slope. Thus for $t_j \leq t < t_{j+1}, \frac{dy}{dt} = F(y(t_j), t_j)$. Starting with our initial condition, $y(a) = y_0$, we approximate y on the interval $[t_0, t_1]$ by the straight line through (y_0, t_0) of slope $F(y_0, t_0)$. This gives $y(t_1) = y_0 + (t_1 - t_0)F(y_0, t_0)$. Then, by assuming $y(t_j) = y_j$, and repeating this process, we get:

$$y_{j+1} = y_j + (t_{j+1} - t_j)F(y_j, t_j). \tag{8.4}$$

To simplify notation we will call $(t_{j+1} - t_j) = h_{j+1}$. Usually we will assume the partition is uniformly spaced and just write h. Then we get $y_{j+1} = y_j + hF(y_j, t_j)$. This formula applies if F is linear or nonlinear, if y is scalar or vector-valued. In the case of a homogeneous system of linear ODEs, since $F(y,t) = Ay$, it gives:

$$y_{j+1} = (I + hA)y_j \tag{8.5}$$

Both (8.4) and (8.5) could also be written (using $t_{j+1} = t_j + h$) as $y(t_j + h) = y(t_j) + hy'(t_j)$. This is a first order Taylor's series approximation for $y(t)$ at t_j; in general $y(t+h) = y(t) + hy'(t) + \frac{h^2}{2}y''(t) + \cdots + \frac{h^n}{n!}y^{(n)}(t)$ is an nth order Taylor's series approximation for y. In the case of linear homogeneous systems of ODEs the Taylor's expansion is easy:

$$y' = Ay, y'' = (y')' = (Ay)' = Ay' = A(Ay) = A^2 y, \cdots, y^{(n)} = A^n y.$$

Thus an nth order Taylor approximation,

$$y(t+h) = \left(I + hA + \frac{h^2}{2}A^2 \cdots + \frac{h^n}{n!}A^n \right) y, \text{ is equivalent to using the nth partial sum}$$

for e^{At}.

The *Improved Tangent* method uses the assumption that the average slope over an interval will usually be closer to the slope at the midpoint of the interval than that at the left endpoint. To approximate the midpoint, we let

$$y_{j+\frac{1}{2}} = y_j + \frac{h}{2}F(y_j, t_j). \tag{8.6}$$

Then

$$y_{j+1} = y_j + hF(y_{j+\frac{1}{2}}, t_j + \frac{h}{2}). \tag{8.7}$$

The *Cauchy-Euler* method uses, rather than the midpoint slope, the average of the slopes at the endpoints. The y value at the right endpoint is first predicted using the Euler method, then corrected. For this reason this method is known as a *predictor-corrector* method. First we get our predictor

$$\overset{*}{y}_{j+1} = y_j + hF(y_j, t_j) \tag{8.8}$$

Then using the predictor value for the right endpoint, we get our approximation to the average slope over the interval $[t_j, t_{j+1}]$. Then our corrected approximation is

$$y_{j+1} = y_j + \frac{h}{2}\left[F(y_j, t_j) + F(\overset{*}{y}_{j+1}, t_{j+1})\right]. \tag{8.9}$$

Higher order Taylor series would be another way of improving our approximation. As we have seen, this presents no particularly difficulty in the linear case. For nonlinear problems, however, the higher derivatives of y are not readily available. Instead, there are several other techniques that can be used to improve Euler's method, some of which we will now consider.

Rather than just guessing that the slope at the endpoint, or the average of slopes at the ends is a good approximation of the average slope over the interval, we could try constructing a formula that would match the Taylor expansion well without using derivatives. For instance we might try a formula that combined a function evaluation at (y_t, t_j) with another at some point found by going for some distance with the correct slope from (y_j, t_j). This would give us a formula such as

$$y_{j+1} = y_j + h\left[w_1 F(y_j, t_j) + w_2 F(y_j + ha_{21}F(y_j, t_i), t_j + hb_2)\right]. \tag{8.10}$$

The labeling of the constants will make more sense when we get to the general case. Now we want to solve for w_1, w_2, a_{21}, and b_2. To do this we expand (8.10) in a Taylor series in h. We need the expansion of

$F(y_j + ha_{21}F(y_j + t_j), t_j + hb_2)$. At $h=0$ we have $F(y_j, t_j)$. Taking $\dfrac{d}{dh}$ gives

$F_y(y_j + ha_{21}F(y_j, t_j), t_J + hb_2)a_{21}F(y_j, t_j) + F_t(y_j + ha_{21}F(y_j, t_j), t_J + hb_2)b_2$ which

at $h=0$ is $a_{21}F(y_j, t_j)F_y(y_j, t_j) + b_2F_t(y_j, t_j)$. Similarly, $\dfrac{d^2}{dh^2}$ at $h=0$ gives

$a_{21}F_{yy}F^2 + 2a_{21}b_2F_{yt}F + b_2^2F_{tt}$. Thus

$$y_{j+1} = y_j + h\Big[(w_1 + w_2)F(y_j, t_j)\Big] + h^2\Big[w_2a_{21}F(y_j, t_i)F_y(y_j, t_j) + w_2b_2F_t(y_j, t_j)\Big].$$

$$+h^3\frac{w_2}{2}\Big[a_{21}F_{yy}F^2 + 2a_{21}b_2F_{yt}F + b_2^2F_{tt}\Big] + 0(h^4) \tag{8.11}$$

Now we consider the Taylor's expansion at

$y(t_j + h) = y(t_j) + hy'(t_j) + \dfrac{h^2}{2}y''(t_j) + \dfrac{h^3}{6}y'''(t_j) + 0(h^4)$.　　We　know　that

$y(t_j) = y_j, y'(t_j) = F(y_j, t_j)$.　By the chain rule $y'(t_j) =$

$\dfrac{d}{dt}y'(t) = \dfrac{d}{dt}F(y_j, t_j) = F_y(y_j, t_j)\dfrac{dy}{dt} + F(y_j, t_j) = F_y(y_j, t_j)F_y(y_j, t_j) + F_t(y_j, t_j)$.

Similarly, $y''(t_j) = F_{yy}F^2 + 2F_{yt}F + F_{tt} + F_y^2F + F_yF_t$. So

$$y_{j+1} = y_j + hF(y_j + t_j) + \dfrac{h^2}{2}\Big[F_y(y_j, t_j)F(y_j, t_j) + F_t(y_j, t_i)\Big] + h^3$$

$$\Big[F_{yy}F^2 + 2F_yF + F_{tt} + f_y^2F + F_yF_t\Big] + 0(h^4) \tag{8.12}$$

If we try to match coefficients between (8.11) and (8.12) we get:

$$O(1): y_0 = y_0$$
$$O(h): w_1 + w_2 = 1$$
$$O(h^2): w_2a_{21} = \frac{1}{2}, w_2b_2 = \frac{1}{2} \tag{8.13}$$

Some of the h^3 terms in (8.12) don't appear at all in (8.11), so we can't match to

third order, but any scheme with $w_1 = 1 = w_2, b_2 = \dfrac{1}{2w_2}, a_{21} = \dfrac{1}{2w_2}$, for any

$w_2 \neq 0$, will work to second order. Letting $w_2 = 1\left(w_1 = 0, b_2 = a_{21} = \frac{1}{2}\right)$ gives the

Improved Tangent method; $w_2 = \frac{1}{2}\left(w_1 = \frac{1}{2}, b_2 = a_{21} = 1\right)$ gives the Cauchy-Euler

method. This process has derived for us what is known as a 2-stage Runge-Kutta scheme. It can be extended to give an m-state Runge-Kutta scheme by setting

$$y_{j+1} = y_j + h\sum_{r=1}^{m} w_r k_r, \quad k_1 = F(y_j, t_j), \tag{8.14}$$

$$k_r = F\left(y_j + h\sum_{s=1}^{r-1} a_{rs}k_s, t_j + hb_r\right)$$

using the constants to match the Taylor expansion. The best known Runge-Kutta method is probably the 4-stage one given by

$$y_{j+1} = y_j + \left(\frac{h}{6}[k_1 + 2k_2 + 2k_3 + k_4]\right),$$

$$k_1 = F(y_j, t_j),$$

$$k_2 = F\left(y_j + \left(\frac{h}{2}\right)k_1, t_j + \frac{h}{2}\right),$$

$$k_3 = F\left(y_j + \left(\frac{h}{2}\right)k_2, t_j + \frac{h}{2}\right),$$

$$k_4 = F\left(y_j + hk_3, t_j + h\right). \tag{8.15}$$

This scheme is fairly easy to implement numerically, since at each step k_i is given as a function of already known values. A scheme with this property is call *explicit*. There are also *implicit* schemes, where at each step you have to solve an equation for the unknown, but we will not consider such schemes here.

EXERCISES

8.1 Show that in 8.10

(a) $w_1 = 0, w_2 = 1, a_{21} = \dfrac{1}{2} = b_2$, gives the Improved Tangent method.

(b) $w_1 = \dfrac{1}{2} = w_2, a_{21} = 1 = b_2$, gives the Cauchy-Euler method.

8.2 Show that for a system of linear homogeneous ODEs, $\dfrac{d\vec{y}}{dt} = A\vec{y}$, both the Improved Tangent and the Cauchy-Euler method are equivalent to a second order Taylor approximation.

8.3 Write computer programs to apply both Improved Tangent and the Cauchy-Euler methods with constant h values, to 2x2 systems of linear ODEs. Write the program so that it allows you to choose h, and the interval. Apply these programs to solve the following.

(a) $\dfrac{d}{dt}\begin{pmatrix} x_1 \\ x_2 \end{pmatrix} = \begin{pmatrix} 2 & -1 \\ 7 & -3 \end{pmatrix}\begin{pmatrix} x_1 \\ x_2 \end{pmatrix} + \begin{pmatrix} 3 \\ -4 \end{pmatrix}$

on the interval [0,3] with $h = \dfrac{1}{10}$, and $\vec{x}(0) = \begin{pmatrix} 2 \\ 3 \end{pmatrix}$.

(b) $\dfrac{d}{dt}\begin{pmatrix} x_1 \\ x_2 \end{pmatrix} = \begin{pmatrix} 0 & 1 \\ -2 & -5 \end{pmatrix}\begin{pmatrix} x_1 \\ x_2 \end{pmatrix} + \begin{pmatrix} 0 \\ 12\sin(t) \end{pmatrix}$

on the interval $\left[0, 2\pi\right]$ with $h = \left[\dfrac{\pi}{12}\right]$, and $\vec{x}(0) = \begin{pmatrix} 0 \\ 0 \end{pmatrix}$.

8.4 Consider the system $\dfrac{d\vec{x}}{dt} = \begin{bmatrix} -1 & 2 \\ 2 & -1 \end{bmatrix}\vec{x}, \vec{x}(0) = \begin{pmatrix} 1 \\ 2 \end{pmatrix}$. Solve it on the interval

$\left[0, 1\right]$ by three methods:

(a) Euler method with $h = \dfrac{1}{20}$.

(b) Euler-Cauchy method with $h = \dfrac{1}{10}$. (These two require about the same amount of calculation)

(c) Exactly, by any method.

Compare the solutions by making a chart that gives the values for the three methods at $t = 0, .2, .4, .6, .8,$ and 1.

8.5 Show that the 4-stage Runge-Kutta method given in equation (8.15), when applied to a system $\dfrac{d\vec{y}}{dx} - A\vec{y}$ is a 4th order Taylor approximation.

8.6 Write a program to apply the 4-stage Runge-Kutta method to a 3x3 system of ODEs, and apply it to

$$\frac{d\vec{y}}{dt} = \begin{bmatrix} 1 & -2 & 0 \\ 3 & -1 & -1 \\ -2 & -1 & 4 \end{bmatrix} \vec{y} + \begin{pmatrix} 1 \\ 0 \\ e^{-t} \end{pmatrix}, \vec{y}(0) = \begin{pmatrix} 1 \\ 0 \\ 0 \end{pmatrix}$$

on the interval $[0,1]$ with $h = \dfrac{1}{10}$.

8.7 Use the 4-stage Runge-Kutta method to solve

$$y' = \sin(y), y(0) = 1 \text{ on } [0, 2] \text{ with } h = \frac{1}{10}.$$

Larger Systems

Up to this point we have dealt almost exclusively with 2×2 systems. Practically speaking, this makes things much easier, but theoretically most of what we have done goes through equally well for larger systems, albeit with more work.

The numerical schemes we have discussed, for instance, require no alterations at all, merely more storage space, and calculations. The substitution method still works, with a few extra steps. As an example, consider

$$
\begin{aligned}
x' &= y - 3z &, \quad x(0) &= 4 \\
y' &= -2x + 3y = 3z &, \quad y(0) &= 0 \\
z' &= -2x - y + z &, \quad z(0) &= -2
\end{aligned}
\tag{9.1}
$$

Solve the first equation for z, get z':

$$
\begin{aligned}
3z &= -x' + y \\
3z' &= -x'' + y'
\end{aligned}
\tag{9.2}
$$

Substitute this into the second and 3 times the third equation; $3z' = -6x - 3y + 3z$:

$$
\begin{aligned}
y' &= -2x + 3y + x' - y = -2x + 2y + x' \\
-x'' + y' &= -6x - 3y - x' + y = -6x - 2y - x'.
\end{aligned}
\tag{9.3}
$$

Use the first of the equations in (9.3) to eliminate y' in the second:

$$
-x'' - 2x + 2y + x' = -6x - 2y - x'
\tag{9.4}
$$

Now solve (9.4) for y and get y':

$$4y = x'' - 2x' - 4x$$
$$4y' = x''' - 2x'' - 4x' \tag{9.5}$$

Plugging this into 4 times the first equation in (9.3), $4y' = -8x + 2(4y) + 4x'$ yields

$$x''' - 2x'' - 4x' = -8x + 2x'' - 4x' - 8x + 4x',$$

$$x''' - 2x'' - 2x' + 16x = 0 \tag{9.6}$$

Now solve this. Set $x = e^{\lambda t}$. We get $\lambda^3 - 4\lambda^2 - 4\lambda + 16 = 0$, so $\lambda = 4, 2,$ or -2. (This can be where things get difficult. We will return to this after finishing the example.) Thus,

$$x = Ae^{4t} + Be^{2t} + Ce^{-2t}$$
$$x' = 4Ae^{4t} + 2Be^{2t} - 2Ce^{-2t}$$
$$x'' = 16Ae^{4t} + 4Be^{2t} + 4Ce^{-2t} \tag{9.7}$$

so $4y = x'' - 2x' - 4x = 4Ae^{4t} - 4Be^{2t} - 4Ce^{-2t}$ and

$$y = Ae^{4t} - Be^{2t} + Ce^{-2t}. \tag{9.8}$$

Now, $3z = -x' + y$, so

$$z = -Ae^{4y} - Be^{2t} + Ce^{-2t} \tag{9.9}$$

Initial conditions give

$$A + B + C = 4$$
$$A - B + C = 0$$
$$-A - B + C = -2 \tag{9.10}$$

So $A = 1, B = 2, C = 1$ and we get

$$x = e^{4t} + 2e^{2t} + e^{-2t}$$
$$y = e^{4t} - 2e^{2t} + e^{-2t}$$
$$z = e^{4t} - 2e^{2t} + e^{-2t} \tag{9.11}$$

Notice that to solve this problem we had to factor a cubic. This is one of the critical differences between 2x2 systems and larger ones. Quadratics we can always factor; higher order polynomials are more problematic. If the coefficients of the polynomial are all integers we know that any rational root of the polynomial is equal to a factor of the constant term divided by a factor of the coefficient on the highest order term. Using this, and long division, we can sometimes factor higher order polynomials. For example, let us find the roots of the fourth polynomial:

$$2x^4 + x^3 - 3x^2 - 8x - 12 = 0 \tag{9.12}$$

We know that any rational root must be a factor of 12: $\pm1, \pm2, \pm3, \pm4, \pm6, \pm12$ divided by 1 or 2. Thus the possible roots are

$$\pm\frac{1}{2}, \pm1, \pm\frac{3}{2}, \pm2, \pm3, \pm4, \pm6, \pm12$$

Trying the integers first we find that $x = 2$ is a solution to (9.12) so $(x - 2)$ is a factor. Long division gives

$$(x - 2)(2x^3 + 5x^2 + 7x + 6) = 0 \tag{9.13}$$

Now repeat the process with $2x^3 + 5x^2 + 7x + 6$. The possible rational roots are: $\pm\frac{1}{2}, \pm1, \pm\frac{3}{2}, \pm2, \pm3, \pm6$. This time none of the integers work, but

$$2\left(\frac{-3}{2}\right)^3 + 5\left(\frac{-3}{2}\right)^2 + 7\frac{-3}{2} + 6 = \frac{-27}{4} + \frac{45}{4} - \frac{42}{4} + \frac{24}{4} = 0.$$

Thus, $\frac{-3}{2}$ is a root, $(2x + 3)$ is a factor. Long division again gives

$$(x - 2)(2x + 3)(x^2 + x + 2) = 0. \text{`} \tag{9.14}$$

The quadratic formula now gives us the other two roots: $x = \frac{-1}{2} \pm i\frac{\sqrt{7}}{2}$.

Unfortunately not all polynomials have rational roots (see the exercises). When this happens we can use a numerical scheme, such as Newton's method, to approximate the roots.

Newton's Method

Newton's Method is a way to approximating the zeros of a differentiable function. We start with an initial approximation to the root, x_0, then construct the tangent to the curve at the point $(x_0, f(x_0))$. If $f'(x_0) \neq 0$, this line will intersect the x axis somewhere, namely at $x_0 - \frac{f(x_0)}{f'(x_0)}$. This becomes the next approximation.

Continue the iteration $x_{j+1} = x_j - \dfrac{f(x_j)}{f'(x_j)}$ until the error is small enough.

Considering again our example (9.1), we can also solve this problem using our eigenvalue-eigenvector techniques. Setting the determinant of $A - \lambda I$ equal to 0 gives:

$$\lambda^3 - 4\lambda^2 - 4\lambda + 16 = 0, \text{ so } \lambda = 4, 2 \text{ or } -2.$$

Notice we have to factor the same cubic again. We find the eigenvectors by Gaussian elimination and get that $\lambda_1 = 4$ gives

$$u_1 = \begin{bmatrix} -1 \\ -1 \\ 1 \end{bmatrix}; \lambda_2 = 2 \text{ gives } u_2 = \begin{bmatrix} -1 \\ 1 \\ 1 \end{bmatrix} \text{ and } \lambda_3 = -2 \text{ gives } u_3 = \begin{bmatrix} 1 \\ 1 \\ 1 \end{bmatrix}.$$

So we let $x(t) = a_1(t)u_1 + a_2(t)u_2 + a_3(t)u_3$. Substituting this into (8.1) gives

$$\frac{da_1}{dt}u_1 + \frac{da_2}{dt}u_2 + \frac{da_3}{dt}u_3 = 4a_1u_1 + 2a_2u_2 - 2a_3u_3$$
(9.15)

and

$$x(0) = a_1(0)u_1 + a_2(0)u_2 + a_3(0)u_3.$$

Note that

$$\begin{bmatrix} 4 \\ 0 \\ -2 \end{bmatrix} = (-1)\begin{bmatrix} -1 \\ -1 \\ 1 \end{bmatrix} + (-2)\begin{bmatrix} -1 \\ 1 \\ 1 \end{bmatrix} + (1)\begin{bmatrix} 1 \\ 1 \\ 1 \end{bmatrix}.$$

This combined with (9.15) and using the linear independence of $u_1, u_2,$ and u_3 gives

$$a'_1 = 4a_1 \ a_1(0) = -1$$
$$a'_2 = 2a_2 \ a_2(0) = -2$$
$$a'_3 = 2a_3 \ a_3(0) = 1 \qquad (9.16)$$

so $a_1 = -e^{4t}, a_2 = -2e^{2t}, a_1 = e^{-2t}$, and

$$x(t) = -e^{4t}\begin{bmatrix} -1 \\ -1 \\ 1 \end{bmatrix} - 2e^{2t}\begin{bmatrix} -1 \\ 1 \\ 1 \end{bmatrix} + e^{-2t}\begin{bmatrix} 1 \\ 1 \\ 1 \end{bmatrix} \tag{9.17}$$

$$= \begin{bmatrix} e^{4t} + 2e^{2t} + e^{-2t} \\ e^{4t} - 2e^{2t} + e^{-2t} \\ -e^{4t} - 2e^{2t} + e^{-2t} \end{bmatrix}$$

which is, of course, the same as (9.11). This problem could also be solved by the solution operator techniques, as follows

$$P = \begin{bmatrix} -1 & -1 & 1 \\ -1 & 1 & 1 \\ 1 & 1 & 1 \end{bmatrix}, P^{-1} = \begin{bmatrix} 0 & -\dfrac{1}{2} & \dfrac{1}{2} \\ -\dfrac{1}{2} & \dfrac{1}{2} & 0 \\ \dfrac{1}{2} & 0 & \dfrac{1}{2} \end{bmatrix}, \text{ and } P^{-1}AP = \begin{bmatrix} 4 & 0 & 0 \\ 0 & 2 & 0 \\ 0 & 0 & -2 \end{bmatrix},$$

so

$$e^{At} = Pe^{Dt}P^{-1} = P\begin{bmatrix} e^{4t} & 0 & 0 \\ 0 & e^{2t} & 0 \\ 0 & 0 & e^{-2t} \end{bmatrix}P^{-1}$$

$$= \begin{bmatrix} \dfrac{1}{2}\left(e^{2t} + e^{-2t}\right) & \dfrac{1}{2}\left(e^{4t} - e^{2t}\right) & \dfrac{1}{2}\left(-e^{4t} + e^{-2t}\right) \\ \dfrac{1}{2}\left(-e^{2t} + e^{-2t}\right) & \dfrac{1}{2}\left(e^{4t} + e^{2t}\right) & \dfrac{1}{2}\left(-e^{4t} + e^{-2t}\right) \\ \dfrac{1}{2}\left(-e^{2t} + e^{-2t}\right) & \dfrac{1}{2}\left(-e^{4t} + e^{2t}\right) & \dfrac{1}{2}\left(e^{4t} + e^{-2t}\right) \end{bmatrix}$$

We can check that $e^{At}\begin{bmatrix} 4 \\ 0 \\ 2 \end{bmatrix}$ again gives (9.11).

The eigenvalue-eigenvector solution techniques can be more complicated, however, in those cases where there are not sufficient eigenvectors to span $\mathbb{R}^n$. If

λ_i is a double root with only one linearly independent eigenvector, we can find a generalized eigenvector the same way as before: if u_i spans the kernel of $A - \lambda_i I$, then let u_{i+1} be a solution (which will exist) of $(A - \lambda_i I)u_{i+1} = u_i$. To illustrate what can happen with roots of multiplicity higher than two, we will consider two examples. First, let

$$A = \begin{bmatrix} -1 & 0 & -4 \\ 1 & 1 & 2 \\ 1 & 0 & 3 \end{bmatrix}. \tag{9.18}$$

Thus $\det(A - \lambda I) = -(\lambda - 1)^3$, so 1 is a triple root. $A - 1$ is

$$\begin{bmatrix} -2 & 0 & -4 \\ 1 & 0 & 2 \\ 1 & 0 & 2 \end{bmatrix} \tag{9.19}$$

and Gaussian elimination gives us that the kernel is spanned by $\begin{bmatrix} -2t \\ s \\ t \end{bmatrix}$. This is a

two-dimensional kernel, but since 1 was a triple eigenvalue, we need three eigenvectors, so we look for a generalized one. When we go to solve, we see that

$$\begin{bmatrix} -2 & 0 & -4 \\ 1 & 0 & 2 \\ 1 & 0 & 2 \end{bmatrix}\begin{bmatrix} a \\ b \\ c \end{bmatrix} = \begin{bmatrix} -2t \\ s \\ t \end{bmatrix} \tag{9.20}$$

is solvable if and only if $s = t$. So we set $s = t = 1$ and get $\phi_1 = \begin{bmatrix} -2 \\ 1 \\ 1 \end{bmatrix}$. Let ψ be

the generalized eigenvector, any solution of (9.20), for instance, $\begin{bmatrix} 1 \\ 0 \\ 0 \end{bmatrix}$. Finally let

ϕ_2 be any regular eigenvector linearly independent of ϕ_1, for instance $s = 1, t = 0$,

giving $\begin{bmatrix} 0 \\ 1 \\ 0 \end{bmatrix}$. Now by setting $P = (\phi_1, \psi, \phi_2)$ we can put A in Jordan canonical form:

$$P^{-1}AP = \begin{bmatrix} 1 & 1 & 0 \\ 0 & 1 & 0 \\ 0 & 0 & 1 \end{bmatrix}. \tag{9.21}$$

For our second example, consider

$$A = \begin{bmatrix} -8 & 7 & -25 \\ 3 & -1 & 8 \\ 4 & -3 & 12 \end{bmatrix} \tag{9.22}$$

Again, $\det(A - \lambda I) = -(\lambda - 1)^3$, so 1 is a triple root. This time, however, the kernel of $A - 1 =$

$$\begin{bmatrix} -9 & 7 & -25 \\ 3 & -2 & 8 \\ 4 & -3 & 11 \end{bmatrix} \tag{9.23}$$

is spanned by $\begin{bmatrix} -2t \\ t \\ t \end{bmatrix}$, so we have only one eigenvector, $\phi = \begin{bmatrix} -2 \\ 1 \\ 1 \end{bmatrix}$. Setting

$(A - I)\psi_1 = \phi$ and solving, gives us a family of solutions of the form

$$\begin{bmatrix} -2t + 1 \\ t + 1 \\ t \end{bmatrix} = t \begin{bmatrix} -2 \\ 1 \\ 1 \end{bmatrix} + \begin{bmatrix} 1 \\ 1 \\ 0 \end{bmatrix}. \tag{9.24}$$

We can get one generalized eigenvector, for instance, $t = 0$ gives $\psi = \begin{bmatrix} 1 \\ 1 \\ 0 \end{bmatrix}$, but

any other vector in the family described by (9.24) would be a linear combination of ϕ and ψ. To get a second generalized eigenvector, we must solve $(A - 1)\psi_2 = \psi_1$. This gives

$$\begin{bmatrix} 3 - 2t \\ 4 + t \\ t \end{bmatrix} = t \begin{bmatrix} -2 \\ 1 \\ 1 \end{bmatrix} + \begin{bmatrix} 3 \\ 4 \\ 0 \end{bmatrix}, \tag{9.25}$$

so let $\psi_2 = \begin{bmatrix} 3 \\ 4 \\ 0 \end{bmatrix}$. Now $P = (\phi, \psi_1, \psi_2)$ gives us the canonical form for A:

$$PAP^{-1} = \begin{bmatrix} 1 & 1 & 0 \\ 0 & 1 & 1 \\ 0 & 0 & 1 \end{bmatrix}.$$

(9.26)

In general, the Jordan form of the matrix is block diagonal, with each block of the form

$$\begin{bmatrix} \lambda & 1 & 0 & \cdots & \cdots & 0 \\ 0 & \lambda & 1 & 0 & \cdots & 0 \\ \vdots & \ddots & \ddots & \ddots & \ddots & \vdots \\ & & \ddots & \ddots & \ddots & 0 \\ \vdots & & & \ddots & \lambda & 1 \\ 0 & \cdots & \cdots & \cdots & 0 & \lambda \end{bmatrix}.$$

If this is $k \times k$, this corresponds to one regular eigenvector ϕ, and a string of generalized eigenvectors $\{\psi_i\}_{i=1}^{k-1}$, defined by

$$(A - \lambda I)\phi = 0$$
$$(A - \lambda I)\psi_1 = \phi$$
$$(A - \lambda I)\psi_j = \psi_{j-1} \quad j = 2, \cdots, k-1.$$

If $k = 1$, we have a regular eigenvector with no generalized eigenvectors associated with it. Now we can proceed to solve, as before.

EXERCISES

9.1 Factor

(a) $6x^4 + 17x^3 - 8x^2 - 13x + 6$

(b) $4x^4 + 12x^3 + 17x^2 + 10x + 2$

9.2 Show that $x^3 - 5x^2 - 3x + 6 = 0$
has no rational roots. Use Newton's method to approximate the roots.

9.3 Solve the following system by substitution.

$$\left[\begin{array}{ll} \dfrac{dx}{dt} = 2x - 2y - 3z & x(0) = 1 \\[2mm] \dfrac{dx}{dt} = -2y - z & y(0) = 1 \\[2mm] \dfrac{dz}{dt} = 5x - 3y - 5z & z(0) = 0 \end{array}\right].$$

9.4 Solve the system in Exercise 9.3 by eigenvectors.

In exercises 9.5-9.7 find $P, P-1$, and put A in canonical form.

9.5 $A = \begin{bmatrix} 2 & 1 & 3 \\ 0 & 2 & 4 \\ 0 & 0 & 2 \end{bmatrix}$.

9.6 $A = \begin{bmatrix} 1 & 2 & 1 \\ 0 & 1 & 1 \\ 0 & 0 & 3 \end{bmatrix}$.

9.7 $A = \begin{bmatrix} -2 & 0 & -1 \\ -1 & -1 & -1 \\ 1 & 0 & 0 \end{bmatrix}$.

9.8 Find e^{At} for the matrix A in exercise 9.3.

9.9 Find e^{At} for the matrix A in exercise 9.7.

CHAPTER

Electrical Systems.

Where might one of these larger systems of differential equations arise? As was the case of 2 x 2 systems, one natural place is the study of electrical circuits. Simple circuits yielded second order systems, and more complex networks will give rise to larger order systems.

In order to set up the equations for a circuit, we will need the voltage drops due to the various circuit elements (see Chapter 5), as well as Kirchoff's first and second laws. Kirchoff's second law, which we have seen earlier (Chapter 5), states that the sum of the voltage drops around any closed loop is equal to the voltage applied in that loop. Kirchoff's first law says the current entering any point is equal to the current leaving the point. Thus, at a node where several wires come together, the sum of the currents entering the node equals the sum of the currents leaving the node. Along a piece of wire with no nodes the current is the same all along the wire, until it comes to a node, Let us see how this works with an example (see Figure 10.1).

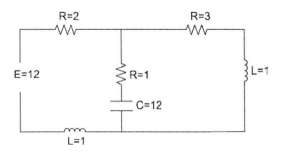

Figure 10.1

First we will define three currents: let I_1 be the current clockwise from node 2 to node 1, I_2 be the current clockwise from node 1 to node 2 and I_3 be the current down from node 1 to node 2 (see Figure 10.2).

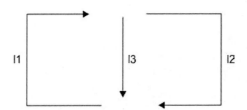

Figure 10.2

As mentioned above, the current is the same all along any of these three pieces of the circuit, by Kirchoff's first law.

The direction chosen for these currents is arbitrary. Choosing I_3 to go up, from node 2 to node 1, for instance, would merely change the sign of I_3 everywhere it appears. If the actual flow of current is in the direction we have chose, I will be positive; otherwise we will get a negative value for I.

Continuing with our example from Figure 10.1, we find we have three closed loops to which we can apply Kirchoff's 2nd law, the left loop (I_1 then I_3), the right loop (I_2 then $-I_3$), and the outside loop I_1 then I_2. These give us, respectively,

$$12 = 2I_1 + I_3 + 2Q_3 + \frac{dI_1}{dt}$$

$$0 = 3I_2 + \frac{dI_2}{dt} + 2(-Q_3) + (-I_3) \tag{10.1}$$

$$12 = 2I_1 + 3I_2 + \frac{dI_2}{dt} + \frac{dI_1}{dt}$$

Notice that the 3rd equation is the sum of the first two. Since the rate of change on a capacitor is the current through the capacitor, we get

$$\frac{dQ_3}{dt} = I_3. \tag{10.2}$$

Also, Kirchoff's 1st law (applied at either node), gives us

$$I_1 = I_2 + I_3. \tag{10.3}$$

Throw out the redundant 3rd equation in (10.1), and use (10.3) to eliminate I_3 to get

$$\frac{dI_1}{dt} = -3I_1 + I_2 - 2Q_3 + 12$$

$$\frac{dI_2}{dt} = I_1 - 4I_2 + 2Q_3$$

$$\frac{dQ_3}{dt} = I_1 - I_2 \tag{10.4}$$

or

$$\frac{d}{dt} = \begin{bmatrix} I_1 \\ I_2 \\ Q_3 \end{bmatrix} = \begin{bmatrix} -3 & 1 & -2 \\ 1 & -4 & 2 \\ 1 & -1 & 0 \end{bmatrix} \begin{bmatrix} I_1 \\ I_2 \\ Q_3 \end{bmatrix} + \begin{bmatrix} 12 \\ 0 \\ 0 \end{bmatrix}.$$ (10.5)

We could have used (10.3) to eliminate one of the other variables instead. This would give us a different system, but the same answer at the end.

Consider another example (See Figure 10.3).

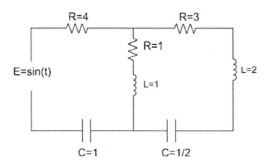

Figure 10.3

Again, we will define I_1, I_2, and I_3 as in Figure 10.2. We get the following system,

$$\sin t = 4I_1 + 2I_2 + 2\frac{dI_2}{dt} + 2Q_2 + Q_1$$

$$0 = 2I_2 + 2\frac{dI_2}{dt} + 2Q_2 - \frac{dI_3}{dt} - I_3$$

$$\frac{dQ_1}{dt} = I_1$$

$$\frac{dQ_2}{dt} = I_2$$

$$I_1 = I_2 + I_3$$ (10.5)

Eliminating $I_3 (I_3 = I_1 - I_2)$, gives

$$\sin t = 4I_1 + 2I_2 + 2\frac{dI_2}{dt} + 2Q_2 + Q_1$$

$$0 = 2I_2 + 2\frac{dI_2}{dt} + 2Q_2 - I_1 + I_2 - \frac{dI_1}{dt} + \frac{dI_2}{dt}$$

$$= I_1 + 3I_2 + 2Q_2 - \frac{dI_1}{dt} + 3\frac{dI_2}{dt}.$$

Solve these for $\dfrac{dI_1}{dt}$ and $\dfrac{dI_2}{dt}$,

$$\frac{dI_2}{dt} = -2I_1 - I_2 - \frac{1}{2}Q_1 - Q_2 + \frac{1}{2}\sin t$$

$$\frac{dI_1}{dt} = -1_1 + 3I_2 + 2Q_2 + 3\frac{dI_2}{dt}$$

$$= -1_1 + 3I_2 + 2Q_2 - 6I_1 - 2I_2 - \frac{3}{2}Q_1 - 3Q_2 + \frac{3}{2}\sin t$$

$$= -7I_1 - \frac{3}{2}Q_1 - Q_2 + \frac{3}{2}\sin t,$$

so we end up with

$$\frac{d}{dt}\begin{bmatrix} I_1 \\ I_2 \\ Q_1 \\ Q_2 \end{bmatrix} = \begin{bmatrix} -7 & 0 & -\frac{3}{2} & -1 \\ -1 & -1 & -\frac{1}{2} & -1 \\ 1 & 0 & 0 & 0 \\ 0 & 1 & 0 & 0 \end{bmatrix}\begin{bmatrix} I_1 \\ I_2 \\ Q_1 \\ Q_2 \end{bmatrix} + \begin{bmatrix} \frac{3}{2}\sin t \\ \frac{1}{2}\sin t \\ 0 \\ 0 \end{bmatrix} \qquad (10.7)$$

More complicated networks give more complicated systems (see Figure 10.4)

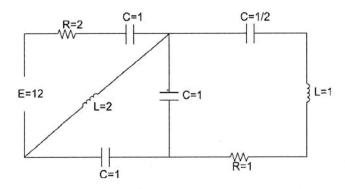

Figure 10.4

Define the currents as in figure 10.5

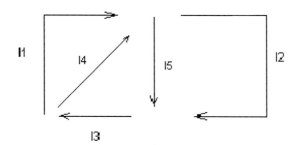

Figure 10.5

Now the outside loop, right loop, and bottom left loop, respectively, give us

$$12 = 2I_1 + Q_1 + 2Q_2 + \frac{dI_2}{dt} + I_2 + Q3$$

$$0 = 2Q_2 + \frac{dI_2}{dt} + I_2 - Q_5$$

$$0 = Q_5 + Q_3 + 2\frac{dI_4}{dt}$$

where

$$\frac{dQ_1}{dt} = I_1, \frac{dQ_2}{dt} = I_2, \frac{dQ_3}{dt} = I_3, \frac{dQ_5}{dt} = I_5 \qquad (10.9)$$

Kirchoff's first law at the nodes give us,

$$I_4 = -I_1 + I_3, I_5 = -I_2 + I_3. \qquad (10.10)$$

Using (10.9) to eliminate I_1 and I_5 we get

$$12 = 2I_1 + 2I_4 + Q_1 + 2Q_2 + \frac{dI_2}{dt} + I_2 + Q3$$

$$0 = 2Q_2 + \frac{dI_2}{dt} + I_2 - Q_5$$

$$0 = Q_5 + Q_3 + 2\frac{dI_4}{dt}$$

where

$$\frac{dQ_1}{dt} = I_3 - I_4, \frac{dQ_2}{dt} = I_2, \frac{dQ_3}{dt} = I_3, \frac{dQ_5}{dt} = -I_2 + I_3.$$

subtracting the second from the first gives

$$12 - 2I_3 - 2I_4 + Q_1 + Q_3 + Q_5.$$

We can use this to eliminate I_3 and solve for $\dfrac{dI_2}{dt}, \dfrac{dI_4}{dt}, \dfrac{dQ_1}{dt}, \dfrac{dQ_2}{dt}, \dfrac{dQ_3}{dt}$, and $\dfrac{dQ_5}{dt}$:

$$\frac{dI_2}{dt} = -I_2 - 2Q_2 + Q_5$$

$$\frac{dI_4}{dt} = -\frac{1}{2}Q_3 - \frac{1}{2}Q_5$$

$$\frac{dQ_1}{dt} = \frac{1}{2}Q_1 - \frac{1}{2}Q_3 - \frac{1}{2}Q_5 + 6$$

$$\frac{dQ_2}{dt} = I_2$$

$$\frac{dQ_3}{dt} = I_4 - \frac{1}{2}Q_1 - \frac{1}{2}Q_3 - \frac{1}{2}Q_5 + 6$$

$$\frac{dQ_5}{dt} = -I_2 + I_4 - \frac{1}{2}Q_1 - \frac{1}{2}Q_3 - \frac{1}{2}Q_5 + 6.$$

So,

$$\frac{d}{dt}\begin{bmatrix} I_2 \\ I_4 \\ Q_1 \\ Q_2 \\ Q_3 \\ Q_5 \end{bmatrix} = \begin{bmatrix} -1 & 0 & 0 & -2 & 0 & 1 \\ 0 & 0 & 0 & 0 & -\frac{1}{2} & -\frac{1}{2} \\ 0 & 0 & -\frac{1}{2} & 0 & -\frac{1}{2} & -\frac{1}{2} \\ 1 & 0 & 0 & 0 & 0 & 0 \\ 0 & 1 & -\frac{1}{2} & 0 & -\frac{1}{2} & -\frac{1}{2} \\ -1 & 1 & -\frac{1}{2} & 0 & -\frac{1}{2} & -\frac{1}{2} \end{bmatrix} \begin{bmatrix} I_2 \\ I_4 \\ Q_1 \\ Q_2 \\ Q_3 \\ Q_5 \end{bmatrix} + \begin{bmatrix} 0 \\ 0 \\ 6 \\ 0 \\ 6 \\ 6 \end{bmatrix} . \tag{10.11}$$

Exercises

Get a system of the form $\dfrac{dx}{dt} = Ax + b$ for each of the following networks.

10.1

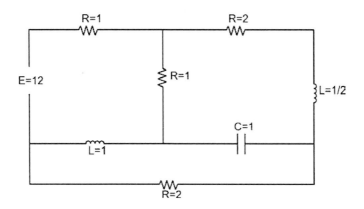

10.2

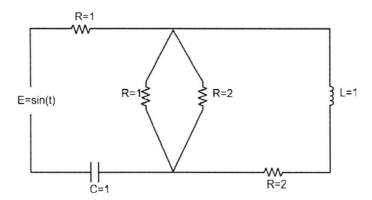

10.3

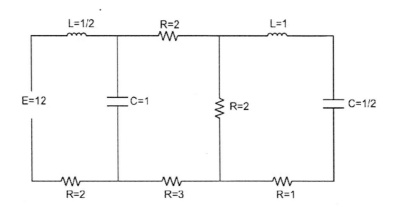

REVIEW QUESTIONS

1. *Solve using eigenvector techniques:*

$$\frac{dx}{dt} = \begin{bmatrix} -1 & -1 \\ 4 & -5 \end{bmatrix} x + \begin{bmatrix} \sin t \\ \cos t \end{bmatrix}; x(0) = \begin{bmatrix} 2 \\ 1 \end{bmatrix}.$$

2. *Find e^{At}.*

    (a) $\begin{bmatrix} -4 & 1 \\ -5 & -2 \end{bmatrix}.$

    (b) $\begin{pmatrix} 1 & -1 & 1 \\ 1 & -2 & 0 \\ -1 & 1 & -1 \end{pmatrix}.$

3. *Use the 4-state Runge-Kutta method with h=0.1 to solve the following initial value problem on the interval [0,10]. Graph y vs. x. (Every 5th point is sufficient if plotting by hand).*

    $$\frac{dx}{dt} = x(1+\cos t - x - y), x(0) = 0.5$$

    $$\frac{dy}{dt} = x(\sin t - x - y), x(0) = 0.5.$$

4. *Solve using eigenvector methods.*

    $$\frac{dx}{dt} = \begin{bmatrix} -3 & 4 \\ -1 & -7 \end{bmatrix} x, x(0) = \begin{bmatrix} 1 \\ 1 \end{bmatrix}.$$

5. *Show that the Cauchy-Euler method applied to $\frac{dy}{dt} = Ay, y(0) = y_0$, is a 2nd order Taylor approximation at each step.*

6. *For scalar valued, first order nonhomogeneous problems, we could use the integrating factor method:*

$$\frac{dy}{dt} = ay(t) + b(t), \; y(0) - y_0$$

gives

$$y(t) = e^{At}\left[\int_0^t e^{-As}\mathbf{b}(s)ds + y_0\right].$$

Show that this formula works and use it to solve:

$$\frac{dx}{dt} = \begin{bmatrix} -1 & 1 \\ -2 & -4 \end{bmatrix} x + \begin{bmatrix} t \\ 1 \end{bmatrix}, \; x(0) = \begin{bmatrix} 1 \\ 2 \end{bmatrix}.$$

$$\left(\text{Hint: } e^{At} = e^{A(-t)}\right)$$

7.   Solve the following system, using eigenvector methods.

$$\frac{dx}{dt} = \begin{bmatrix} 1 & -1 \\ -4 & 1 \end{bmatrix} x + \begin{bmatrix} e \\ e^{-t} \end{bmatrix}, \; x(0) = \begin{bmatrix} 1 \\ 1 \end{bmatrix}.$$

8.   Find e^{At}.

(a) $A = \begin{bmatrix} 2 & -1 \\ 2 & 0 \end{bmatrix}$

(b) $A = \begin{bmatrix} -4 & 1 \\ -1 & -2 \end{bmatrix}.$

9.   Solve $\dfrac{dx}{dt} = \begin{bmatrix} 6 & 2 \\ 2 & 3 \end{bmatrix} x + \begin{bmatrix} t \\ 2 \end{bmatrix}; \; x(0) = \begin{bmatrix} 3 \\ -1 \end{bmatrix}.$

10.   Use the 4-stage Runge-Kutta method with $h = 0.1$ to solve the
following initial value problem on $[0,1]$.

$$\frac{dx}{dt} = \begin{bmatrix} 2 & -1 \\ 2 & 0 \end{bmatrix} x + \begin{bmatrix} 1 \\ 2 \end{bmatrix}; \; x(0) = \begin{bmatrix} 1 \\ 3 \end{bmatrix}.$$

11. Find the system of ODE's (in the form $\dfrac{dx}{dt} = Ax + b$) for the circuit

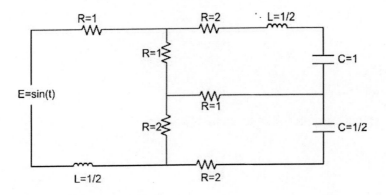

12. Solve for $I(t), Q(t)$ if $I(0) = 0 = Q(0)$.

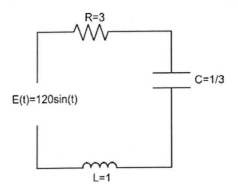

13. Solve using either the eigenvectors or the solution operator method:

$$\frac{dx}{dt} = \begin{bmatrix} -5 & 6 \\ -3 & 1 \end{bmatrix} x, \, x(0) = \begin{bmatrix} 2 \\ 1 \end{bmatrix}.$$

14. Solve:

$$\frac{dx}{dt} = \begin{bmatrix} 2 & -1 \\ 2 & 5 \end{bmatrix} x + \begin{bmatrix} r(t) \\ 0 \end{bmatrix}; \, x(0) = \begin{bmatrix} 0 \\ 1 \end{bmatrix}.$$

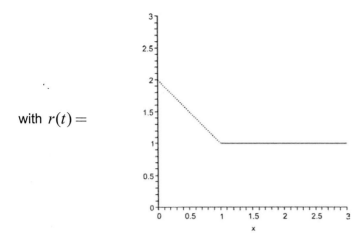

with $r(t) =$

15. Find e^{At} for

$$A = \begin{bmatrix} -2 & 1 & 0 & 1 \\ 0 & -1 & 0 & -1 \\ 0 & 1 & -2 & 1 \\ 0 & -1 & 0 & -1 \end{bmatrix}.$$

16. Solve:

$$\frac{dx}{dt} = 2x = 2y + 1$$

$$\frac{dy}{dt} = 5x - 4y + r(t), \quad x(0) = 1, y(0) = -1.$$

for $r(t) =$

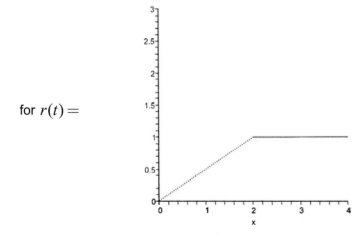

17. Find $Q(t), I(t)$ for the given circuit. Use any method.

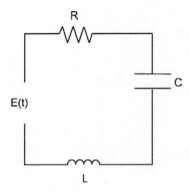

a) $R = 4, L = 2, C = \dfrac{1}{4}, E(t) = 0, I(0) = 1, Q(0) = 2.$

b) $R = 5, L = 1, C = \dfrac{1}{6}, E(t) = \sin t, I(0) = 1, Q(0) = 0.$

PART II

Nonlinear Systems of
Ordinary Differential
Equations

CHAPTER

Limited Growth

To this point we have been concentrating on linear problems. A great many situations can be described by linear equations, but these models are usually only valid under certain limited conditions. For a simple example, let us consider the problem of the growth of a single population. It seems reasonable to say that the rate of growth for the population will depend on the population size; the more individuals available to give birth, the faster the population will increase. The simplest model of this form would be to say that the rate of change of the population is proportional to the number of individuals. This gives us the linear model:

$$\frac{dy}{dt} = cy, \tag{11.1}$$

where c is the constant of proportionality. The solution is

$$y(t) = Ae^{ct}, \tag{11.2}$$

where A can be determined if we know the value of y at some initial time. For certain populations, such as bacteria with an ample food supply, this solution is a good match for reality, at least for a while. However, if this growth rate were to continue, we would have a population growing without bound. In fact, if growth were to continue at the maximum rate, a single bacterium of E. Coli would produce a ton of E. Coli in fifty hours. Clearly, this cannot be correct. For one thing, the food supply will run out, for another, in many species, excessive crowding will lower the birth rate.

How can we include these effects in our model? One rational way is to assume the food supply to be constant, enough to feed a certain population size, say K individuals. If the population somehow gets bigger than K the food supply will be inadequate, and more will starve than are being born. Thus we want $\dfrac{dy}{dt}$ to equal $f(y)$, a function such that $f(y) < 0$ for $y > K$, $f(0) = 0$ and for y small f is approximately equal to cy. The simplest function that does all this is

$$\frac{dy}{dt} = cy\left(1 - \frac{y}{K}\right); \quad c, K \text{ positive constants.} \tag{11.3}$$

We can solve this by separation of variables:

$$-c\,dt = \frac{-dy}{y\left(1 - \dfrac{y}{K}\right)} = \frac{K\,dy}{y(y - K)} = \left(\frac{1}{y - K} - \frac{1}{y}\right)dy,$$

so

$$-ct + b = \ln|y - k| - \ln|y| = \ln\left|\frac{y - K}{y}\right|,$$

and

$$\frac{y - K}{y} = Ae^{-ct}.$$

Thus

$$y(t) = \frac{K}{1 - Ae^{-ct}} \tag{11.4}$$

with $y_0 = y(0) = \dfrac{K}{1 - A}$, which gives $A = 1 - \dfrac{K}{y_0}$.

As long as the denominator does not go through zero, the limit as t approaches infinity of $\dot{y}(t)$ is K. The denominator will go through zero at a positive time if and only if $A > 1$. For $y_0 > K, 0 < A < 1$ and $y(t)$ approaches K from above. For $0 < y_0 < K, A < 0$ and $y(t)$ approaches K from below. For $y_0 = 0$ or K, $\dfrac{dy}{dt} = 0$ and the solution is a constant.

Physically $y_0 < 0$ doesn't make sense for a population problem. Mathematically it gives $A > 1$, so at some finite $t > 0, 1 - Ae^{-ct} = 0$ and y is unbounded. Thus we see that for any reasonable starting value the population settles down at K, the carrying capacity.

Let us consider another example, this time adding immigration at a constant rate, i.e., $\dfrac{dy}{dt}$ will have limited growth term as in (11.3) which represents the growth of the population due to births minus deaths, plus a constant which represents a constant flux of new individuals in the area. This gives

$$\frac{dy}{dt} = cy\left(1 - \frac{y}{K}\right) + M.$$

(11.5)

This problem has too many constants. In order to eliminate some, we will nondimensionalize. First we identify the units of each term; y and K have units of individuals, or biomass, or some measure of population. One natural unit of measurement for population is the fraction of the carrying capacity of the environment. Let $x = \dfrac{y}{K}$,

then x will be a dimensionless quantity, equal to the fraction of the carrying capacity. Substituting this into (11.5), we get $\dfrac{dx}{dy} = cx(1 - x) + \dfrac{m}{K}$. Since x is dimensionless, $\dfrac{dx}{dt}$ has units of $\dfrac{1}{time}$. The intrinsic growth rate for x near zero is cx, which also must have units $\dfrac{1}{time}$. If we replace t with the dimensionless $T = ct$ we get $\left(\text{since } \dfrac{dx}{dt} = \dfrac{dx}{dT}\dfrac{dT}{dt} = c\dfrac{dx}{dT}\right)$

$$\frac{dx}{dT} = x(1 - x) + \frac{m}{Kc}.$$

Now rename $\dfrac{m}{Kc} = p$. Thus we have

$$\frac{dx}{dT} = x(1 - x) + p,$$

(11.6)

which is equivalent to (11.5) with

$$x = \frac{y}{K}, T = ct, p = \frac{m}{Kc}.$$

(11.7)

Let us consider, without loss of generality, (11.6). We could solve (11.6) by separation of variables as we did in (11.3). This will be left as an exercise. Instead, let us consider possible values to which x could settle down. If $\dfrac{dx}{dT} = f(x)$ and

x is approaching a constant $x*$, then, $\dfrac{dx}{dt}$ must be approaching zero. This tells

us that $\lim\limits_{x \to x^*} f(x) = 0$, and if f is continuous, $f(x^*) = 0$. In (11.6) f is a

polynomial, thus continuous. Therefore, the only constant values that x can

approach are roots of the right hand side, i.e., solutions to $-x^2 + x + p = 0$. The

roots are $\dfrac{1 \pm \sqrt{1 + 4p}}{2}$. If p is positive (which would be the case if it represented

a net immigration), this gives two real roots, one negative, and thus irrelevant to

our problem, and the other, call it $x*$, positive; in fact >1. We can see that $\dfrac{dx}{dt}$ is

positive for $0 < x < x*$ and negative for $x > x*$. In fact for f continuous this is

sufficient to prove that x approaches $x*$.

Theorem 11.1

Let be a solution to $x' = f(x)$, f continuous. Suppose there is an $x*$ in $[a,b]$ such that
$f(x^*) = 0, f(x) > 0$ for $a \le x < x^*, f(x) < 0$ for $x^* < x \le b$. If $x(0)$ is in $[a,b]$,
$\lim\limits_{t \to \infty} x(t) = x*$.

Proof

Due to the sign of f, $x(t)$ cannot move away from $x*$ as t increases, so if $x(t)$

does not approach $x*$ it must be bounded away from $x*$. Now, by the

fundamental theorem of calculus

$$x(t) = x(0) + \int_0^t x'(s)ds. \tag{11.8}$$

If $x(t)$ is bounded away from $x*$, then by continuity of f, $x'(t) = f(x)$ is

bounded away from zero. Assume $x(t) < c < x*$ for all t. Then there is some

$h > 0$ such that $f(x) \ge h$, so $\dfrac{dx}{dt} \ge h$ for all t. But then $x(t) = x(0) + \int_0^t x'(s)ds$

$> x(0) + \int_0^t h\,ds = x(0) + ht$, so $\lim\limits_{t \to \infty} x(t) > \lim\limits_{t \to \infty}[x(0) + ht] = \infty$. This is a

contradiction; $x(t) < c < x*$. Similarly if $x(t) > d > x*$, then $f(x) < -h$, so

$x(t) \leq x(0) - ht,$ which gives $\lim_{t\to\infty} x(t) = -\infty,$ another contradiction; $x(t) > d > x^*.$

Therefore $x(t)$ cannot be bounded away from x^*; $\lim_{t\to\infty} x(t) = x^*.$

For p positive, then, the population tends to $\dfrac{1+\sqrt{1+4p}}{2}$ times the carrying capacity of the environment. This is more than the carrying capacity, but is possible, since though more individuals are dying than being born, (i.e., $y > K$), immigration makes up the difference.

If instead of immigration we consider emigration or harvest at a fixed rate, we get equation (11.6) again, this time with $p < 0.$ If $p > -\dfrac{1}{4}, 0 < 1 + 4p < 1,$ so the roots $\dfrac{1 \pm \sqrt{1+4p}}{2},$ call them x_+ and x_-, are both real, positive, and between 0 and 1. We see that x' is positive for $x_- < x < x_+$ and negative for $x < x_-$ or $x > x_+.$ Thus if $x(0)$ is in $(x, x_-),$ $x(t)$ approaches $x_+.$ If $x(0) < x_-,$ the population decreases and eventually the model fails (you can't harvest more than the total population). Mathematically the solution decreases without bound.

If $p < -\dfrac{1}{4},$ there are no roots, $f(x)$ is always negative and bounded away from zero. For any initial condition the solution is monotone decreasing, without bound.

For this example we were able to find the roots of f exactly, by hand, but for some this won't be possible. For instance consider

$$y' = -y^3 + 3y - 1. \tag{11.9}$$

We need the roots of the equation

$$f(y) = -y^3 + 3y - 1 = 0. \tag{11.10}$$

First we sketch f. The derivative of f is $-3y^2 + 3,$ so $f' = 0$ at 1 and –1; $f(1) = 1, f(-1) = -3.$ Also $f(-2) = 1, f(2) = -3,$ so there are three real roots: one between –2 and –1, one between –1 and 1, one between 1 and 2.

Now use Newton's Method (see Chapter 9) to approximate the solution. If you know there is exactly one root in some interval $[a,b]$, a good initial guess is the midpoint $\cdot \dfrac{a+b}{2}$.

For $x_0 = 1.5$ we get $x_1 = -2.0667, \cdots, x_4 = x_5 = -1.8794; x_0 = 0$ gives $x_3 = x_4 = \cdots = .3473; x_0 = 1.5$ gives 1.5321. Now $f(x) > 0$ for $x - 1.8794; f(x) < 0$ for $-1.8794 < x < .3473; f(x) > 0$ for $.3473 < x < 1.5321$; and $f(x) < 0$ for $x > 1.5321$. Thus if $x(0) < .3473, x(t)$ approaches -1.8794; if $x(0) > .3473, x(t)$ approaches 1.5321; $x(t)$ equal to the constant .3473 (approximately) is also a solution.

Exercises

11.1 Solve (11.6) by separation of variables for the following values of p :

(a) 2   (b) .01   (c) -.01   (d) $-\dfrac{1}{4}$ (e) -2

(in parts b) and c) approximate the roots if you like).

Using the theorem in this section, what can you say about the $t = \infty$ limits of solutions to the following problems?

11.2 $y' = y(1 - y)(1 + y)$.

11.3 $y' = \sin y$.

11.4 $y' = e^y + e^{-y} - 3 - y$, (find the roots numerically).

11.5 Given that N has units of grams/milliliter, non dimensionalize

$$\frac{dN}{dt} = \left(\mu \frac{C - N}{K + C - N} - D \right) N.$$

What can you say about the limit as $t \to \infty$? (Assume all constants are >0.)

Two Specie Interactions

Another factor to be taken into account when considering a species' growth rate is that species' interaction with other species. Two of the main forms of this interaction are predator- prey systems and competitive systems.

Considering predator-prey systems first, imagine a population of wolves and rabbits on an island with an unlimited supply of clover. The rabbits eat the clover and multiply (as rabbits will, given a chance). If there were no wolves, the rabbit population would grow, taking the simplest, linear growth model:

$$\frac{dR}{dt} = aR \ .$$

Wolves, on the other hand, do not eat clover. In the absence of rabbits the wolves will starve:

$$\frac{dW}{dt} = -bW \ .$$

Now we add interaction, wolves <u>do</u> eat rabbits. Again taking a simple model, we assume the rate at which rabbits get eaten will be proportional to the number of meetings between rabbits and wolves. This will be jointly proportional to the number of rabbits and the number of wolves. In the same way, the rate at which wolves eat will be proportional to the product of R and W. Thus

$$\frac{dR}{dt} = aR - cRW \qquad = R(a - cW)$$

$$\frac{dW}{dt} = -bW + dRW \quad = W(dR - b) \tag{12.1}$$

where a, b, c, and d are positive constants. Now we can nondimensionalize by letting

$$u = \frac{dR}{b}, v = \frac{cW}{a}, k = \frac{b}{a}, \text{ and } t' = at. \tag{12.2}$$

This gives

$$\frac{du}{dt} = u(1-v)$$

$$\frac{dv}{dt} = kv(u-1). \tag{12.3}$$

This set of equations is known as the *Volterra-Lotka* equations. Volterra formulated them in 1926 to describe a predator-prey system for two species of fish in the Adriatic Sea. Lotka had come up with the same set of equations in 1920 to model the evolution of the concentrations of the intermediate compounds X and Y in the following chemical reaction:

$$\begin{array}{lcl} A+X & k_1 & 2X \\ & \rightarrow & \\ A+Y & k_2 & 2Y \\ & \rightarrow & \\ Y & k_3 & B \\ & \rightarrow & \end{array} \tag{12.4}$$

where k_1, k_2 and k_3 are rate constants and the concentrations of the reactant A and the product B are held constant.

The growth rates given in system (12.3) are functions only of the current population levels; time does not appear explicitly in the equations, only in the derivative, $\frac{d}{dt}$. Such a system is said to be autonomous. This is an important distinction. In an autonomous system the labeling of some time as $t = 0$ is a mere convention. For instance, if u_1, v_1 are solutions to (12.3) with $u_1(0) = u_0, v_1(0) = v_0$ and u_2, v_2 are solutions to the same system of equations but with initial conditions $u_2(3) = u_0, v_2(3) = v_0$ then u_1, v_1 and u_2, v_2 will trace out exactly the same curve in the uv plane, only 3 time units part. Further, two solutions to an autonomous system, plotted in the uv plane, cannot cross. The easiest way to see this is to eliminate t from the equations as follows.

Consider the autonomous system

$$\frac{dx}{dt} = f(x, y)$$

$$\frac{dy}{dt} = g(x, y) \tag{12.5}$$

By the chain rule $\dfrac{dy}{dx} = \dfrac{\frac{dy}{dt}}{\frac{dx}{dt}}.$ Applying this to (12.5) we get

$$\frac{dy}{dx} = \frac{g(x, y)}{f(x, y)}. \tag{12.6}$$

The slope through any point in the x,y plane is thus uniquely defined unless $g(x_0, y_0) = 0 = f(x_0, y_0)$. Such a point is called a critical point. Solutions cannot cross at a non critical point due to the uniqueness of solutions to initial value problems. At a critical point $\frac{dx}{dt} = 0 = f(x_0, y_0)$ and $\frac{dy}{dt} = 0 = g(x_0, y_0)$ so (x_0, y_0) is a constant solution.

If we again consider (12.3), we can eliminate t, getting

$$\frac{dv}{du} = \frac{kv(u-1)}{u(1-v)}. \tag{12.7}$$

This can actually be solved by separation of variables:

$$\frac{(1-v)}{v} dv = \frac{k(u-1)}{u} du,$$

so $\ln v - v = ku - k \ln u + c,$ or

$$\ln v + k \ln u - ku - v = c. \tag{12.8}$$

We can get some information from this (for instance u and v must stay bounded) but it's not very easy to picture the solution.

Another way of dealing with a system of nonlinear equations, is to linearize the system about the critical points. To do this we first need to find the critical points. For our example (12.3) this means solving

$$u(1-v) = 0$$
$$kv(u-1) = 0 \tag{12.9}$$

This has two critical solutions: $u = 0, v = 0$ and $u = 1, v = 1$. Now, for each critical point (u_0, v_0), let $u = u_0 + \varepsilon u_1, v = v_0 + \varepsilon v_1$, where ε is small. First, with $(u_0, v_0) = 0, 0$, we substitute $u = \varepsilon u_1, v = \varepsilon v_1$ into (12.3) and get

$$\varepsilon \frac{du_1}{dt} = \varepsilon u_1 \left(-\varepsilon v_1 \right)$$

$$\varepsilon \frac{dv_1}{dt} = k\varepsilon v_1 \left(\varepsilon u_1 - 1 \right).$$

canceling one ε gives

$$\frac{du_1}{dt} = u_1 \left(1 - \varepsilon v_1 \right)$$

$$\frac{dv_1}{dt} = kv_1 \left(\varepsilon u_1 - 1 \right).$$

If our solution is close to the critical point, ε is small and can be ignored. Setting $\varepsilon = 0$ gives the linear system:

$$\frac{du_1}{dt} = u_1$$

$$\frac{dv_1}{dt} = kv_1. \tag{12.10}$$

This gives u increasing exponentially and v approaching zero exponentially.

Next we set $u = 1 + \varepsilon u_1, v = 1 + \varepsilon v_1$ and get

$$\varepsilon \frac{du_1}{dt} = (1 + \varepsilon u_1)(-\varepsilon v_1)$$

$$\varepsilon \frac{dv_1}{dt} = k(1 + \varepsilon v_1)(\varepsilon u_1),$$

so after canceling ε and letting go to zero, we need to solve

$$\frac{du_1}{dt} = -v_1$$

$$\frac{dv_1}{dt} = ku_1. \tag{12.11}$$

This system has eigenvalues $\pm i\sqrt{k}$. The solutions are ellipses.

What does this tell us about the solution to the full nonlinear system (12.3)? for u, v very near a critical point, the solution will be close to the solution to the linearization, so near $(0,0)$ u will be increasing, v decreasing. Since these solutions will not stay close to (0,0), the solution to this linearization is valid only for a short time. Near (0,0) solutions will be close to ellipses, but what does this mean? Will they be closed loops, spiraling in, spiraling out? In general this is not easy to determine. For our example, we can tell by looking at the exact solution (12.8). If we fix a v value and try to solve for u, we have to solve an equation of the form

$$\ln u - u = A \tag{12.12}$$

This will have exactly two solutions for $A < -1$, one for $A = -1$, none otherwise (see figure (12.1)).

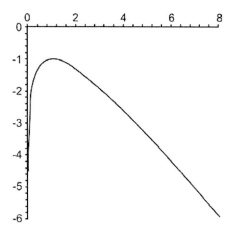

Figure 12.1

Similarly, if we fix u and solve for v we get an equation of the same form. This eliminates the possibility of spirals and tells us our solutions will be closed loops. A combination of linearization and isocline methods gives us a fairly good picture of our solutions. We can plot solutions in the u, v phase plane and by going back to (12.3) can determine the direction in which the curve is being traced out as t increases. (See figure 12.2.)

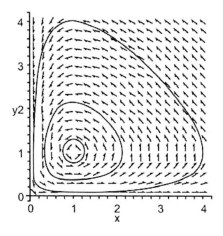

Figure 12.2

This method of determining that solutions were closed loops was possible only because we had an exact solution.

Next let us consider a predator-prey system where, in the absence of predators, the prey obey a limited growth model. Again using a simple interaction, we get

$$\frac{dR}{dt} = R(a - eR - cW)$$

$$\frac{dW}{dt} = W(dR - b) \tag{12.13}$$

which is the same as (12.1) except for the $-eR^2$ term in $\dfrac{dR}{dt}$. Our substitutions this time will be

$$u = \frac{eR}{a}, v = \frac{cW}{a}, t = aT, A = \frac{d}{e}, B = \frac{da}{be}. \tag{12.14}$$

we get

$$\frac{du}{dt} = u(1 - u - v)$$

$$\frac{dv}{dt} = Av(u - B). \tag{12.15}$$

This system has three critical points: $(u,v) = (0,0), (1,0)$, or $(B, 1-B)$. We linearize around each of these, and get, respectively,

$$\frac{du_1}{dt} = u_1$$

$$\frac{dv_1}{dt} = ABv_1 \tag{12.16a}$$

eigenvalues 1, $-AB$, and eigenvectors $\begin{bmatrix} 1 \\ 0 \end{bmatrix}, \begin{bmatrix} 0 \\ 1 \end{bmatrix}$,

$$\frac{du_1}{dt} = -u_1 - v_1$$

$$\frac{dv_1}{dt} = -A(1 - B)v_1 \tag{12.16b}$$

eigenvalues 1, $(1 - B)$, and eigenvectors $\begin{bmatrix} 1 \\ 0 \end{bmatrix}, \begin{bmatrix} 1 \\ -1 - A(1 - B) \end{bmatrix}$,

$$\frac{du_1}{dt} = -Bu_1 - Bv_1$$

$$\frac{dv_1}{dt} = -A(1-B)u_1,$$

(12.16c)

eigenvalues $\dfrac{-B \pm \sqrt{B^2 - 4AB(1-B)}}{2}$.

If B is greater than one, it says that even if the rabbit population is at carrying capacity there aren't enough rabbits to support a wolf population (with u=1, $\dfrac{dv}{dt} < 0$). Also in this case we see that there is no critical point with $v > 0$. We will consider $B < 1$. In that case both (12.16a) and (12.16b) have one positive and one negative eigenvalue, so near these points, there is one direction along which solutions are moving toward the critical point, and one in which solutions are moving (exponentially) away from the critical point. The third critical point (11.16c) has either two negative real eigenvalues, or a pair of complex conjugate roots with negative real part. Thus anything starting close to this critical point will move closer, in the case of complex roots, spiraling in.

We know that for solutions starting sufficiently close to $(B, 1-B)$, (u,v) will actually approach $(B, 1-B)$, but we do not know how close to sufficiently close. It turns out (as we will see later) that any solution with $u(0) > 0$ and $v(0) > 0$ eventually approaches $(B, 1-B)$.

The predator-prey systems we have considered this far have had per capita growth rates $\left(\dfrac{1}{u}\dfrac{du}{dt} \text{ and } \dfrac{1}{v}\dfrac{dv}{dt}\right)$ that were linear functions of u and v. This made finding the steady states easy. For more general systems there is a variety of numerical schemes available. One such is the *generalized Newton's method.*

Generalized Newton's Method

To solve $f(x) = 0$ where $f : \mathbb{R}^n \to \mathbb{R}^n$ has continuous first derivatives in all variables, we first make an initial guess, x_0. Newton's method is the iterative scheme

$$x_{j+1} = x_j - J^{-1}(x_j)f(x_j)$$

(12.17)

where $J^{-1}(x_j)$ is the inverse of J, the Jacobian, evaluated x_j, that is

$$\left(J(x_j)\right)_{k,l} = \frac{\partial f_k}{\partial x_l}(x_j)$$

(12.18)

It is often easier to solve

$$J(x_j)k_{j+1} = J(x_j)x_j - f(x_j) \tag{12.19}$$

by Gaussian elimination at each step.

For the 2x2 systems we are now considering, it is probably easiest to find $J(x)$ in general, invert it by hand, and use (12.17).

We will analyze predator-prey systems with nonlinear growth rates in general later.

Another form of interaction between two species is competition for a common resource. The presence of one species reduces the growth rate of the other by reducing the available resource. Starting with two species following limited growth rates, and adding the interaction in the simplest way, we get a system of the form

$$\frac{dx}{dt} = x(a - bx - cy)$$

$$\frac{dy}{dt} = y(d - ex - fy), \tag{12.20}$$

all constants positive. In the exercises you will consider the various cases of this system. Again, competitive systems with nonlinear per capita growth rates can also be considered.

EXERCISES

In numbers 12.1-12.3 use the Cauchy-Euler method with h=0.2 and 100 steps, i.e., for $t = 0$ to 20. Sketch the resulting curve (plot every tenth point if plotting by hand).

12.1
$$\frac{du}{dt} = u(1 - v)$$
$$\frac{dv}{dt} = \frac{1}{4}v(u - 1),$$

where $(u(0), v(0))$ is a) $(2,1)$ and b) $\left(\frac{1}{2}, \frac{1}{2}\right)$

12.2
$$\frac{du}{dt} = u(1 - u - v)$$
$$\frac{dv}{dt} = v(u - 1)$$

where $(u(0), v(0)) = (0.4, 0.6)$.

$$\begin{aligned} \frac{du}{dt} &= u(1 - u - v) \\ 12.3 \quad \frac{dv}{dt} &= \frac{1}{4}v\left(u - \frac{1}{3}\right) \end{aligned}$$

where $(u(0), v(0)) = \left(\frac{1}{2}, \frac{1}{2}\right)$.

In Exercises 12.4 and 12.5 find the critical points. Linearize about each and sketch a couple of typical solutions to the linearization about each critical point. Using some other color, sketch in what you think a solution to the full nonlinear problem might look like.

$$\begin{aligned} \frac{dx}{dt} &= x(1 - x - y) \\ 12.4 \quad \frac{dy}{dt} &= \frac{1}{4}y(1 + x - 2y). \end{aligned}$$

$$\begin{aligned} \frac{dx}{dt} &= 2y - x \\ 12.5 \quad \frac{dy}{dt} &= -y + 2x(1 - x). \end{aligned}$$

12.6 Consider system 12.20. Using the carrying capacity of one species in the absence of the other as the natural measure, nondimensionalize x and y. The intrinsic growth rate of x $\left(\frac{1}{x}\frac{dx}{dt}\text{ for } x \text{ and y both very small}\right)$ provides a natural time scale. Nondimensionalize the system.

12.7 In exercise 12.6 you should have ended up with a system in the form

$$\begin{aligned} \frac{du}{dt} &= u(1 - u - \alpha v) \\ \frac{dv}{dt} &= \gamma v(1 - \beta u - v). \end{aligned}$$
(12.21)

Analyze these cases.

(a) $\alpha, \beta < 1$

(b) $\alpha, \beta > 1$

(c) $\alpha < 1 < \beta$

(Recall that all the parameters are positive.) For each case find steady states and the eigenvalues of the linearization about each. What can you say about solutions near each steady state?

12.8 In system (12.21) (Exercise 12.7) sketch solutions to the following cases:

(a) $\alpha = \dfrac{1}{3}, \beta = \dfrac{1}{2}, \gamma = 1$

(b) $\alpha = \dfrac{4}{3}, \beta = \dfrac{3}{2}, \gamma = 1$

First sketch the solution to the linearization near each steady state. Then, in another color, sketch some solutions to the full nonlinear problem.

Critical Points

A great deal of information about the solutions to an autonomous system of nonlinear equations can be obtained by study of the critical points or steady states. There are several possibilities for the behavior of the linearized system at a critical point. Let us examine these possibilities for the 2X2 case.

After linearizing, we have a 2X2 linear homogeneous system for u_1 and v_1. (Homogeneous since $u = u_0, v = v_0$ is a solution, so if $u = u_0 + \varepsilon u_1$, and $v = v_0 + \varepsilon v_1$, then $u_1 = 0, v_1 = 0$ is a solution.) The eigenvalues to this system can be unequal and real, complex conjugates, or a double real root.

First consider the case of unequal real roots. There are five possibilities both positive, both negative, one positive and one negative, or one zero the other positive or negative. If both are positive, suppose $0 < \lambda_1 < \lambda_2$ and let u_1 and u_2 be the corresponding eigenvectors. The solution to the linearization is

$$c_1 e^{\lambda_1 t} u_1 + c_2 e^{\lambda_2 t} u_2. \tag{13.1}$$

Since $\lambda_1 < \lambda_2$, for large t this looks like $c e^{\lambda_2 t} u_2$ (unless $c_2 = 0$), and for t large negative it looks like $c_1 e^{\lambda_2 t} u_1$ (unless $c_1 = 0$). (See figure 13.1). Such a critical point is called an <u>unstable node</u>. Sufficiently close to the critical point, solutions to the nonlinear system will have the same general appearance.

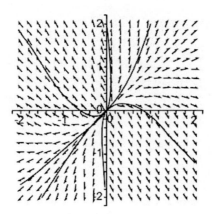

Figure 13.1

If, $\lambda_2 < \lambda_1 < 0$, the solution to the linearization is again given by equation (13.1), and the solution will look the same with the arrows reversed. This is called a <u>stable node</u>, and again sufficiently close to (u_0, v_0) solutions to the nonlinear system will look the same.

If $\lambda_1 < 0 < \lambda_2$ the solution is still given by equation (13.1), but now we will have one solution which approaches (u_0, v_0) along a straight line as t increases $\left(c_1 e^{\lambda_1 t} u_1\right)$ and one which moves straight away from (u_0, v_0), $\left(c_2 e^{\lambda_2 t} u_2\right)$. Other solutions may approach for a while, then move away (see figure 13.2). Eventually all solutions except $\left(c_1 e^{\lambda_1 t} u_1\right)$ become unbounded as t gets large. This is called a <u>saddle point</u>,

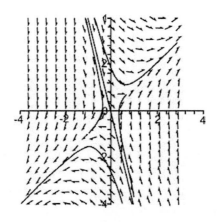

Figure 13.2

and again the solution to the nonlinear system will have the same general appearance, although the solutions moving to, or directly away from the critical point (known as separatrices) (singular: separatrix) may no longer be straight lines. They <u>will</u> still exist.

In the other two cases for unequal real roots, one of the eigenvalues is zero, so solutions are of the form:

$$\left(c_1 u_1 + c_2 e^{\lambda_2 t} u_2\right)$$ (13.3)

If $\lambda_2 > 0$, this will be a constant vector plus a growing multiple of another vector (see figure 13.3). If $\lambda_2 < 0$, the solution will look the same as figure 13.3, but with the arrows reversed. The linearization actually has a whole line of critical points, all the multiples of u_1. Unless the nonlinear part also has a whole curve of critical points, the linearization will not tell us much about the nonlinear problem. Solutions near the critical point might look like either a node or a saddle point, or something else strange, depending on the nonlinear terms.

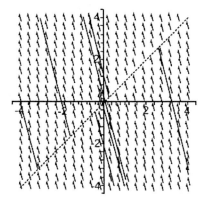

Figure 13.3

For the case of complex conjugate eigenvalues there are three possibilities; the real part can be positive, negative, or zero. If $\lambda = \alpha \pm i\beta$ are the roots and w_1 and w_2 are the associated eigenvectors the solution is

$$c_1 e^{(a+i\beta)t} w_1 + c_2 e^{(a-i\beta)t} w_2,$$

where $c_2 = conj(c_1)$ and $w_2 = conj(w_1)$. Using Euler's formula we can put this in the form

$$e^{\alpha t}\left[(A\cos\beta t + B\sin\beta t)u + (B\cos\beta t - A\sin\beta t)v\right],$$ (13.4)

where everything is real. The real vectors u and v are related to the complex eigenvector w_1 by $w_1 = u + iv$. This equation (13.4) can also be put in the form

$$Ce^{\alpha t}\sin(\beta t + d)u + De^{\alpha t}\cos((\beta t + d)v$$ (13.5)

by the use of trigonometric identities. The part of (13.4) in the square brackets represents an ellipse. Thus if α is negative, solutions spiral in (see figure 13.4) and if α is positive, solutions spiral out with increasing t (see figure 13.4 with the arrows reversed). These cases are known as <u>stable</u> and <u>unstable spiral points</u> respectively. Solutions to the nonlinear problem will look basically the same near the critical point. The spirals can actually be clockwise or counterclockwise.

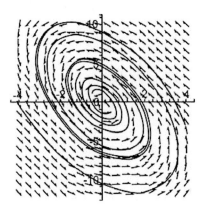

Figure 13.4

In the case $\alpha = 0$, solutions of the form (13.5) are ellipses (see figure 13.5). This case is known as a <u>center</u>. Solutions to the nonlinear problem can be closed loops or spiral in or out, depending on the nonlinear terms. Note that in all cases the solutions can again go around in either direction as t increases, depending on the particular problem.

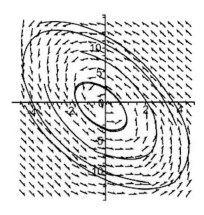

Figure 13.5

We will split the case of equal real roots into two subcases, each with three possibilities. First suppose we have λ, a double eigenvalue, and the matrix is diagonalizable. We have seen that in this case the matrix is λI. Two linearly independent eigenvectors are $\begin{bmatrix} 1 \\ 0 \end{bmatrix}$ and $\begin{bmatrix} 0 \\ 1 \end{bmatrix}$. Solutions are

$$c_1 e^{\lambda t}\begin{bmatrix} 1 \\ 0 \end{bmatrix} + c_2 e^{\lambda t}\begin{bmatrix} 0 \\ 1 \end{bmatrix} = \begin{bmatrix} c_1 \\ c_2 \end{bmatrix}e^{\lambda t}. \tag{13.6}$$

We see that the ratio of x to y is constant. For $\lambda < 0$ solutions move toward the critical point along straight lines (see figure 13.6). For $\lambda > 0$ solutions will move away from the critical point along straight lines (see figure 13.6 with the arrows reversed). These are known as _stable_ and _unstable foci_ or _focus points_. Solutions to the full nonlinear problem will look approximately the same nearby, though they may spiral in, or all come in tangent to a particular direction. If, however, the linearization is a stable focus point, the solution near the critical point _will_ approach the critical point.

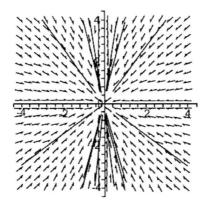

Figure 13.6

A diagonalizable 2X2 matrix with a double zero eigenvalue is just the zero matrix. Any constant is a solution to the linearization. This tells us basically nothing about the solution to our nonlinear problem.

Finally we consider the case of a matrix with a double eigenvalue of λ, but only a single eigenvector u_1 and a generalized eigenvector u_2. The solution to the linearization (see chapter 6) will be of the form

$$(c_1 + c_2 t)e^{\lambda t}u_1 + c_2 e^{\lambda t}u_2. \tag{13.7}$$

Notice that for any c_2 not zero the coefficient on u_1 goes through zero for exactly one value of t. Also the line spanned by u_1 is a solution, but the line spanned by u_2 is not. For λ positive the coefficient on u_2 is always growing is absolute value, while the coefficient on u_1 changes sign.

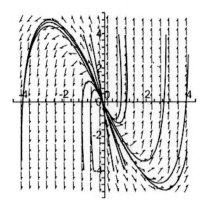

Figure 13.7

This is known as an unstable, *improper node*. For $\lambda < 0$ we have the same picture with the arrows reversed. This would be a stable improper node. Solutions to the nonlinear problem will look much the same near the critical point, although again they may spiral in (or out) or not all cross u_2 the crucial aspect of stable or unstable remains the same.

The final possibility is a matrix with a double eigenvalue of zero and only one eigenvector. The solution will have the form

$$(c_1 + c_2 t)\mathsf{u}_1 + c_2\mathsf{u}_2. \tag{13.8}$$

Any multiple of u_1 is a constant solution $(c_2 = 0)$. All other solutions will be straight lines parallel to u_1 (see figure 13.8). Not much can be said about the solution to the nonlinear problem, unless it also has a whole line of critical points.

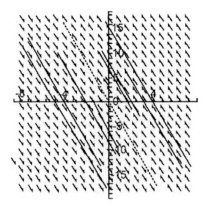

(Figure 13.8)

In some of these cases we could predict the local behavior of the nonlinear problem from the linearization, in some we could partially predict the nonlinear behavior, at least up to stability, and in some cases the linearization told us almost nothing.

The linearizations that told us the least all were the cases where λ or the real part of λ was equal to zero. Sufficiently small changes in a positive number still give positive numbers; small changes in a negative number give negative numbers, but small changes in zero can give you either.

The other linearizations that only gave partial information about the nonlinear problem, were those with double roots. Since the eigenvalues are roots of a real polynomial, they must either be real or complex conjugates. A double real root, though, is close to either. The double root of a is close to $a \pm \varepsilon i$ as well as close to $a \pm \varepsilon$. Thus small changes in a double root can lead to unequal real roots or complex conjugates. We do, at least, know that for small changes, the new roots will have real part the same sign as the original double root (unless the double root was zero).

Properties that persist under small changes in the problem are known as _generic_. Properties that may change with arbitrarily small variations in the problem are _non-generic_. Thus having a proper node, a spiral point or a saddle point are generic properties; having a center, an improper node, or a zero eigenvalue are non-generic.

This may be clearer if we consider how the eigenvalues of a 2X2 matrix depend on the entries of the matrix. Consider the matrix

$$A = \begin{bmatrix} a & b \\ c & d \end{bmatrix}. \tag{13.9}$$

The eigenvalues of A satisfy $(a - \lambda)(d - \lambda) - bc = 0$, or

$$\lambda^2 - Tr(A)\lambda + \det(A) = 0. \tag{13.10}$$

Thus the eigenvalues are

$$\lambda = \frac{Tr(A) \pm \sqrt{Tr(A)^2 - 4\det(A)}}{2}. \tag{13.11}$$

The sum of the eigenvalues is the trace, and the product is the determinant. If the determinant is negative the roots will be real and of opposite sign; we have a saddle point. One of the eigenvalues will be zero if and only if $\det(A) = 0$.

If $\det(A) > 0$, but less than $\dfrac{\left(Tr(A)\right)^2}{4}$, we have unequal real roots: proper nodes.

If $\det(A) = \dfrac{\left(Tr(A)\right)^2}{4}$, λ is a double real root: improper nodes or foci.

If $\det(A) > \dfrac{(tr(A))^2}{4}$ we get complex conjugate roots with real part $= \dfrac{(Tr(A))}{2}$.

Thus $Tr(A) > 0$: unstable spiral points; $Tr(A) < 0$: stable spiral points; $Tr(A) = 0$: centers.

If we plot all this in $\det(A)$ vs. $T(A)$ parameter space (see figure 13.9), we can see that the generic properties occur in open sets of the plane, while the nongeneric properties occur on curves or points. Small changes in the coefficients of A produce small changes in $\det(A)$ and $Tr(A)$ so sufficiently small changes in your matrix will not affect a generic property, but may completely change a nongeneric one.

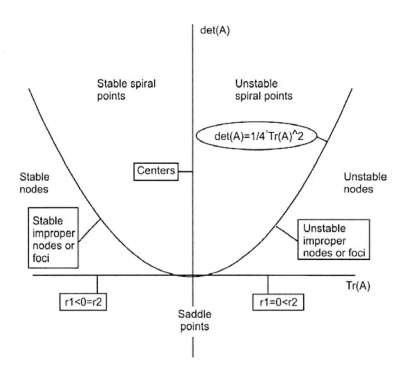

Figure 13.9

Another way of looking at the nongeneric types is as dividing cases between the generic.

For instance consider the matrix

$$B = \begin{bmatrix} c & 1 \\ -1 & c \end{bmatrix},$$

(13.12)

as c changes slowly from -1 to 1. The eigenvalues are $c \pm i$, so B goes from having a stable spiral to a center to an unstable spiral. As c approaches 0 from below the inward spirals are slower and slower until at $c = 0$, they no longer spiral in at all, but form closed loops. As c becomes, positive, the solution starts spiraling out, slowly for c near zero, then more rapidly.

EXERCISES

13.1 The origin $(0,0)$ is the steady state for the system $\dfrac{dx}{dt} = Ax$. Find 2×2 matrices,

A, illustrating the 14 possibilities for a linearized system. For each of these, find

the solution with $x(0) = \begin{bmatrix} a \\ b \end{bmatrix}$, and sketch some typical solution curves.

13.2 Find, linearize about, and identify the type of the steady states for

(a) $\dfrac{d}{dt} \begin{bmatrix} w \\ \theta \end{bmatrix} = \begin{bmatrix} -w - 7\sin\theta \\ w \end{bmatrix}$,

(b) $\dfrac{d}{dt} \begin{bmatrix} x \\ y \end{bmatrix} = \begin{bmatrix} 2x - x^2 - xy \\ xy^2 - 2y \end{bmatrix}$,

(c) $\dfrac{d}{dt} \begin{bmatrix} x \\ y \end{bmatrix} = \begin{bmatrix} x + y^3 - 6y^2 + 9y - 8 \\ -3y + x \end{bmatrix}$.

sketch solutions.

13.3 Consider the family of problems

$$\dfrac{d}{dt} \begin{bmatrix} x \\ y \end{bmatrix} = \begin{bmatrix} 1 & -c \\ 1 & -3 \end{bmatrix} \begin{bmatrix} x \\ y \end{bmatrix},$$

as c goes from 0 to 5. Plot the path in the $\det A, Tr(A)$ plane. Sketch solutions just before, at, and just after, any transition points.

13.4 Repeat problem 13.3 for $\dfrac{dx}{dt} = Bx$ with $B = \begin{bmatrix} 1 & b \\ 1-b & -3 \end{bmatrix}$,

as b goes from 0 to 3.

CHAPTER

Poincaré-Bendixon Theorem

Examining the linearization of a nonlinear system tells us much about the behavior of solutions near critical points. If we want information on the global behavior of solutions, we will need other techniques. To understand these techniques we will first need two concepts; that of a limit set, and that of an invariant set.

Consider the trajectories in the x, y plane of solutions to

$$\frac{dx}{dt} = f(x, y)$$

$$\frac{dy}{dt} = g(x, y). \tag{14.1}$$

Since this is an autonomous system, trajectories cannot intersect. As $t \to \infty$, the trajectories may, among other possibilities, become unbounded, approach a critical point, or approach a closed loop, called a *limit cycle* (see Figure 14.1).

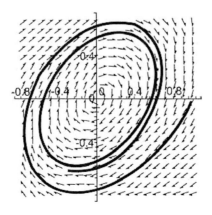

Figure 14.1

The idea of a trajectory approaching a curve is clear, but how do we define it? We can define a trajectory becoming unbounded: $\lim_{t\to\infty}\left[x^2(t)+y^2(t)\right]=\infty$ or approaching a point (a,b): $\lim_{t\to\infty}\left[(x(t)-a)^2+(y(t)-b)^2\right]=0$, but how do we define the situation in figure 14.1? Again our definition will be a statement about limits, although we must be more careful, since limits of $x(t)$ or $y(t)$ as t approaches infinity do not exist. The trajectory in figure 14.1 is not getting and staying close to any point on the closed loop; however, if we follow the trajectory far enough, we get closer and closer to each point. In other words, for any point on the limit cycle, and for any $\varepsilon>0$, if we go far enough out on the trajectory, there will be a point of the trajectory within ε of that point on the limit cycle. Stated formally, we have

Definition (**Limit Set**) A point (a,b) is said to be in the <u>limit set</u> at ∞ of a point (x_0,y_0), if there is an increasing sequence of t values $\{t_j\}_{j=1}^{\infty},t_j\to\infty$ as $j\to\infty$, such that if $(x(t),y(t))$ is the solution to system (14.1), starting at (x_0,y_0), then $\lim_{j\to\infty}(x(t_j),y(t_j))=(a,b)$.

(We could also define limit sets at $t=-\infty$). The collection of all such points is the limit set of (x_0,y_0).

Clearly a critical point is its own limit set, since the trajectory through a critical point is just the critical point itself. Every trajectory that stays bounded has a limit set, which must be closed. To see this, take any increasing unbounded sequence of t values, $\{t_n\}_{n=1}^{\infty}$. This gives an infinite, bounded (since the trajectory is bounded) set of points $\{(x(t_n),y(t_n))\}$, which must have a convergent subsequence. The limit of the convergent subsequence is in the limit set of the trajectory.

The proof that limit sets are closed is left as an exercise.

Clearly, if two points are on the same trajectory, they have the same limit set. Thus, we can refer to the limit sets of points, or of trajectories.

Definition (**Invariant Set**) A set W is said to be invariant under the flow defined by (14.1), if for any point (a,b) in W, the trajectory $(x(t),y(t))$ that goes through (a,b), is in W for all t. If $(x(t_0),y(t_0))=(a,b)$ implies $(x(t),y(t))$ is in W for all $t\geq t_0$, W is said to be positively invariant; if $(x(t),y(t))$ is in W for $t\leq t_0$, W is said to be negatively invariant.

Any solution trajectory is invariant. If W is positively invariant, then the limit set at infinity of any point in W must be in $cl(W)$, the closure of W. A limit set itself will always be invariant.

In three or higher dimensions, limit sets can have many different forms. In two-space, however, there are essentially only three possibilities. The limit set can be a critical point, a limit cycle (as in Figure 14.1), or a set of critical points connected by trajectories. A trajectory from one critical point to another approaches the first as $t \to \infty$ and the other as $t \to -\infty$. (See Figure 14.2).

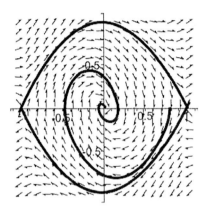

Figure 14.2

This gives us an important result: if W is a bounded, closed, positively invariant set that does not contain a critical point, there will be a limit cycle in W. This result – which is only true in 2 dimensions – is known as the Poincaré-Bendixon theorem.

As an example of how this works, consider the Van der Pol equation,

$$x'' - x'(1 - (x')^2) + x = 0,$$

or putting it in system form,

$$\frac{dx}{dt} = y$$

$$\frac{dy}{dt} = -x + y - y^3. \tag{14.2}$$

The only critical point is $(0,0)$, and the linearization there gives

$$\frac{dx_1}{dt} = \begin{bmatrix} 0 & 1 \\ -1 & 1 \end{bmatrix} x_1. \tag{14.3}$$

The eigenvalues are $\dfrac{1}{2} \pm i\dfrac{\sqrt{3}}{2}$, so the origin is an unstable spiral point.

Sketching the zero slope and vertical isoclines gives us Figure 14.3. Draw the lines shown in Figure 14.4. Solutions can only cross the vertical and horizontal lines, and the short pieces of the cubic, going into the region. If b is sufficiently large, the slope of a solution crossing the lines of slope minus one through $(0,b)$ and $(0,-b)$ will also have to be going into the region (See Exercise 14.4). Thus we have a positively invariant set. The limit set at infinity of any point inside this set is in the closure of the set. Since the only critical point is an unstable spiral point, no trajectory can approach the critical point as $t \to \infty$, so by Poincaré-Bendixon there must be a periodic orbit.

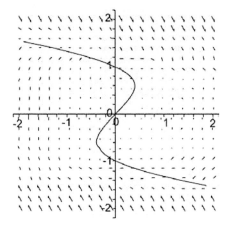

Figure 14.3

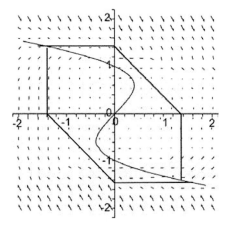

Figure 14.4

Another fact that helps in analyzing solutions, is that the region of attraction for a stable critical point (proper node, spiral, focus, or improper node), is an open set. This means, that if the critical point is the limit set of (a,b), it is also the limit set of all points sufficiently close to (a,b). The same can be said for the region of attraction at $t = -\infty$ for unstable nodes or spiral points. The region of attraction (at either $t = \infty$ or $t = -\infty$) for a saddle point is a curve: the separatrix.

The region of attraction for a limit cycle like the one in Figure 14.2 is either open, or bounded by the limit set itself.

If a trajectory forms a closed loop, there must be a critical point inside the loop. The reason for this can be seen by considering the interior of the loop. Since trajectories cannot cross (throughout we are assuming autonomous systems), this is an invariant set. If there are other closed loops in this set, consider the one surrounding the least area, (if there is no positive lower bound on the area surrounded, the family of closed loops shrinks to a point; a critical point). The interior is again an invariant set. Consider the limit set at infinity of a point in this set. If this limit set contains a critical point, we are done. If not, since there is only one closed loop in the closure of the set, by Poincaré-Bendixon the limit set must be the limit cycle that forms the boundary. Now consider the limit set at $t \to -\infty$. Since trajectories cannot cross, this limit set cannot be the same limit cycle. There are no other closed loops, so the limit set must contain a critical point.

Using all these facts, we can get quite a bit of information about solution curves. Although we do not get an exact solution, we can get rigorous results about the asymptotic behavior of the solution. This is often all we need, and in fact is sometimes of more interest than an exact solution in an inconvenient form.

We can sometimes get information about whole families of systems. For instance, the predator-prey systems we considered in Chapter 12 had linear per capita growth rates $\left(\dfrac{1}{u}\dfrac{du}{dt} \text{ and } \dfrac{1}{v}\dfrac{dv}{dt} \right)$. A more general system such as

$$\frac{du}{dt} = uf(u,v)$$

$$\frac{dv}{dt} = vg(u,v) \tag{14.4}$$

might be considered a predatory-prey system, if it met certain biologically reasonable conditions. We expect an increase in predators to decrease the growth rate of the prey, and an increase in prey to increase the growth rate of the predators. This implies (if u is the prey, v the predator),

$$\frac{\partial f}{\partial v} < 0, \frac{\partial g}{\partial u} > 0. \tag{14.5}$$

If there is a carrying capacity, u_1, for the prey, such that $f(u,v) < 0$ for $u > u_1$, and some level of predators v_1 that number of prey could support, so that $g(u_1, v_1) = 0$, then the region $0 \le u \le u_1, 0 \le v \le v_1$ is a positively invariant set.

Further conditions are necessary before we can apply Poincaré-Bendixon. Some sufficient conditions are, that both species are adversely affected by crowding and that there is some minimum number of prey required to support any predators at all, and a number of predators sufficient to consume prey at the prey's maximum growth rate. These conditions,

$$\frac{\partial f}{\partial u} < 0, \frac{\partial g}{\partial v} < 0.$$

(14.6)

and there exist u_2 and $v_2 < v_1$ such that

$$f(0, v_2) = 0, \quad g(u_2, 0) = 0$$

are enough to make $(0,0)$ and $(u_2, 0)$ unstable steady states $((0,0)$ an unstable node, $(u_2, 0)$ a saddle point), and to guarantee the existence of exactly one other critical point. If this coexistence steady state is unstable, there will be a periodic orbit.

This is a very simplified version of a theorem by Kolmogorov. A nice discussion of the theorem and the biological meaning of the conditions can be found in <u>Mathematical Models in Biology</u> by Leah Edelstein-Keshet. (L. Edelstein-Keshet, Mathematical Models in Biology, The Random House/Birkhäuser Mathematics Series, 1987).

Exercises:

14.1 Prove that a limit set is closed. Let (a^*, b^*) be in the closure of the limit set of a point (x_0, y_0). This implies there are points $\left\{(a_j, b_j)\right\}_{j=1}^{\infty}$, each in the limit set of (x_0, y_0), such that $\lim_{j \to \infty}(a_j, b_j) = (a^*, b^*)$.

Now construct a sequence of t values, as in the definition of a limit point, that approach (a^*, b^*).

14.2 Prove that if (a, b) is in the limit set of (x_0, y_0), so is the trajectory through (a, b).

14.3 Use exercise 14.2 to show that a limit set is invariant.

14.4 In Figure 14.3, the line segment of slope -1 in the first quadrant is $x + y = b, y \geq 0$. Determine b such that on that line $\dfrac{dy}{dx} = \dfrac{-x + y - y^3}{y}$ is less than -1.

the results in the x, y plane.

14.6 Find an invariant region and use Poincaré-Bendixon to show the existence of a periodic orbit for

$$\frac{du}{dt} = v$$

$$\frac{dv}{dt} = (1 - u^2)v - u.$$

14.7 Repeat Exercise 14.5 for the system in Exercise 14.6.

Liapunov Functions

Consider the motion of a pendulum with a bob of mass m on a rigid rod of length r. Let θ be the angle (in radians) that the rod makes with the vertical. Positive θ will mean counterclockwise motion. (See figure 15.1.)

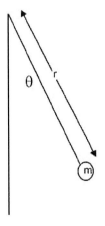

Figure 15.1

Newton's 2nd law says that mass times acceleration equals the sum of the applied forces, where acceleration is the second time derivative of displacement. For our problem, displacement is along the arc of a circle of radius r, thus displacement is $r\theta$. What forces do we have? We will consider two, gravity and friction. Friction, as usual, will be taken to be proportional to velocity (the time derivative of displacement) and in the opposite direction. Thus

$$F_f = -c\frac{d(r\theta)}{dt} \tag{15.1}$$

where $c \geq 0$ (units: [mass]/[time]) is the constant on proportionality.

The force due to gravity is mg, but for our problem, not all of this force affects the motion. For instance, where the bob is straight down, gravity produces no tendency to move. We want the component of F_g tangent to the direction of motion. The component parallel to the rod, i.e., that which is perpendicular to the motion, is balanced by tension in the rod (We could have considered tension as a separate force; this is equivalent). Since gravity is vertical, the component tangent to the motion is $mg \sin \theta$. (See Figure 15.2).

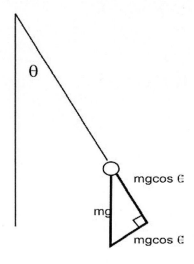

Figure 15.2

Thus, since gravity works toward $\theta = 0, 2\pi$, we get

$$F_g = -mg \sin \theta, \tag{15.2}$$

Now put these together and get

$$m \frac{d^2(r\theta)}{dt^2} = -c \frac{d(r\theta)}{dt} - mg \sin \theta, \tag{15.3}$$

or, since r is a constant

$$mr \frac{d^2(\theta)}{dt^2} = -cr \frac{d(\theta)}{dt} - mg \sin \theta. \tag{15.4}$$

In order to put this in system form we introduce a new variable $\Omega = \dfrac{d\theta}{dt}$. Now we have

$$\frac{d\Omega}{dt} = -\frac{c}{m} \Omega - \frac{g}{r} \sin \theta$$
$$\frac{d\theta}{dt} = \Omega. \tag{15.5}$$

This system has critical points at $\omega = 0, \theta = k\pi, k$ an integer. The linearization at $\big((0, k\pi)\big)$ is

$$\frac{d}{dt}\begin{pmatrix} \dot{\omega}_1 \\ \theta_1 \end{pmatrix} = \begin{bmatrix} -\dfrac{c}{m} & -\dfrac{g}{r}(-1)^k \\ 1 & 0 \end{bmatrix}\begin{bmatrix} \omega_1 \\ \theta_1 \end{bmatrix},$$

so for k odd the eigenvalues are given by

$$\lambda^2 + \frac{c}{m}\lambda - \frac{g}{r} = 0,$$

$$\lambda = -\frac{c}{2m} \pm \sqrt{\frac{c^2}{4m^2} + \frac{g}{r}}.$$

This gives one positive and one negative root; a saddle point. For k even, the eigenvalues are given by

$$\lambda^2 + \frac{c}{m}\lambda + \frac{g}{r} = 0,$$

$$\lambda = -\frac{c}{2m} \pm \sqrt{\frac{c^2}{4m^2} - \frac{g}{r}}.$$

For $c > 0$, this gives either 2 negative reals $\left(\text{if } c^2 \geq \dfrac{4m^2 g}{r}\right)$, or a pair of complex

conjugates with negative real part. Thus we have either a stable node or stable

spiral point. $\left(\text{For } c = 0 \text{ we get } \lambda = \pm i\sqrt{\dfrac{g}{r}}, \text{ a center.}\right)$

The linearization tells us, that if we start sufficiently close to $(0, 2\pi)$, the trajectory will approach $(0, 2\pi)$. It does not tell us how close is sufficiently close. An invariant set, if we could find one, would give us more information, such as that solutions starting in the invariant set say bounded, but would still leave questions. For example, are there limit cycles? Do all solutions stay bounded? What happens to trajectories that do not start close to a stable critical point? The methods we have developed thus far cannot answer this sort of question about global behavior. To get some further insight to our example, let us consider the energy of the system.

The total energy of the system is given by the kinetic energy plus the potential energy. Kinetic energy is given by

$$E_k = \frac{1}{2}mv^2, \tag{15.7}$$

where v is velocity, and potential energy by

$$E_p = mgh,\tag{15.8}$$

where h is the height the mass is raised above some arbitrary datum. We will set the zero datum to be the height the bob is above its location at the straight down position. For our problem, $v = \dfrac{d(r\theta)}{dt} = r\Omega$, and $h = r(1 - \cos\theta)$ (see figure 15.3).

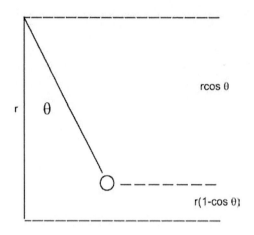

rcos θ

r(1-cos θ)

Figure 15.3

Thus,

$$E(\omega, \theta) = mgr(1 - \cos\theta) + \frac{1}{2}mr^2\omega^2.\tag{15.9}$$

Notice that $E \geq 0, E = 0$ only when $\omega = 0$, and $\theta = 2n\pi$.

If $\big(\omega(t), \theta(t)\big)$ represents a solution to (14.5), then along that curve the energy E can be thought of as a function of t. Using the chain rule, we get

$$\frac{dE}{dt} = \frac{\partial E}{\partial \theta}\frac{d\theta}{dt} + \frac{\partial E}{\partial \omega}\frac{d\omega}{dt}\tag{15.10}$$

so that

$$\begin{aligned}
\frac{dE}{dt} &= mgr\sin\theta\frac{d\theta}{dt} + mr^2\omega\frac{d\omega}{dt}\\
&= mgr\sin\theta\omega + mr^2\omega\left(-\frac{c}{m}\omega - \frac{g}{r}\sin\theta\right)\\
&= mgr\sin\theta\omega - cr^2\omega^2 - mrwg\sin\theta\\
&= -cr^2\omega^2.
\end{aligned}$$

If $c > 0$, i.e., if there is friction, $\dfrac{dE}{dt}$ is negative along trajectory curves, so the energy must decrease as time increases. This already eliminates the possibility of limit cycles; a trajectory can never return to the same point in w, θ space, since $E(w, \theta)$ is decreasing. Sketching the level curves of E is instructive when trying to answer the other questions posted above. (See Figure 15.4).

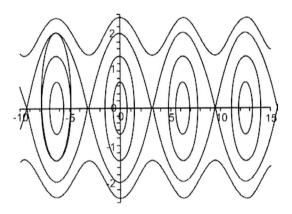

Figure 15.4

The top and bottom curves have $E > 2mgr$; the curves that intersect along the axis have $E = 2mgr$; the closed loops have $E < 2mgr$; and $E = 0$ at $w = 0, \theta = 0, \pm 2\pi, \cdots$ etc. Along the θ axis $(w = 0)$, $0 \leq E \leq 2mgr$.

Since $\dfrac{dE}{dt} = -cr^2w^2$, and $E \geq 0$, trajectories cannot be bounded away from the line $w = 0$ (recall the proof to Theorem 11.1). Thus, a solution must either approach a critical point $(0, k\pi)$, or hit the axis eventually. If the trajectory hits the axis, $E < 2mgr$, and now the trajectory is trapped inside the region bounded by the $E = 2mgr$ curves. This is an invariant set. Since there are no limit cycles, the trajectory must approach the stable critical point. Thus for $c > 0$, all trajectories, except the stable separatrices to the saddle points, approach one of the $(0, 2n\pi)$ critical points.

For $c = 0$, we have $\dfrac{dE}{dt} = 0$, so E is constant along trajectories, and the level curves of E (see figure 15.4) are the solutions.

The function $E(w, \theta)$ in this problem is an example of a Liapunov function. A.M. Liapunov was a Russian mathematician and engineer who, in his 1892 doctoral dissertation, proved the following:

Theorem 15.1 Let x_0 be a critical point of the autonomous system

$$\frac{dx}{dt} = f(x) \tag{15.10}$$

Let $V : \mathbb{R}^n \to \mathbb{R}$ is a continuous function defined on some neighborhood U of x_0, differentiable on $U - \{x_0\}$, such that $V(x_0) = 0$, $V(x) > 0$ for $x \neq x_0$ and $\nabla V(x) \cdot f(x) \leq 0$. Then x_0 is stable. If $\nabla V(x) \cdot f(x) < 0$ for $x \neq x_0$, then trajectories actually approach x_0.

It is not, in general, easy to find Liapunov functions. Sometimes the physics (or biology, etc.) of the problem gives us some natural function to try, as in our example. If not, we can try non-negative functions that are zero at the critical point, and see if we can make them work (e.g., try something of the form $a(x - x_0)^2 + b(y - y_0)^2$, and adjust a and b to make it work).

One important class of differential systems for which the Liapunov function is easily found is *gradient systems*, systems of the form

$$\frac{dx}{dt} = -\nabla F(x), \tag{15.11}$$

where $F : \mathbb{R}^n \to \mathbb{R}$ is a continuous function. In this case F itself, or F plus a constant, is a Liapunov function, since $\dfrac{dF}{dt}$ along solutions is

$$\nabla F \cdot \frac{dx}{dt} = \nabla F \cdot (-\nabla F)$$
$$= -\nabla F \cdot \nabla F$$
$$= -\|\nabla F\|^2$$

Thus any local minimum of F is a stable critical point. For example, consider

$$\frac{dx}{dt} = 3x^2 + 2y$$
$$\frac{dy}{dt} = -2y + 2x. \tag{15.12}$$

This is minus the gradient of $F = y^2 - x^3 - 2xy$.

$$\frac{\partial F}{\partial t} = \frac{\partial F}{\partial x}\frac{dx}{dt} + \frac{\partial F}{\partial y}\frac{dy}{dt}$$
$$= (-3x^2 - 2y)(3x^2 + 2y) + (2y - 2x)(-2y + 2x)$$
$$= -(3x^2 + 2y)^2 - (2y - 2x)^2 \leq 0.$$

The critical points are at

$$\frac{dx}{dt} = 0 = \frac{dy}{dt},$$

or

$$3x^2 + 2y = 0$$
$$-2y + 2x = 0 \tag{15.13}$$

The second equation gives $x = y$. Substituting this into the first gives $3x^2 + 2x = 0$. The roots are $x = 0$ or $-\frac{2}{3}$, so the critical points are $(0,0)$ and $\left(-\frac{2}{3}, -\frac{2}{3}\right)$.

The matrix of the linearization at $(0,0)$ is

$$\begin{bmatrix} 0 & 2 \\ 2 & -2 \end{bmatrix} \tag{15.14}$$

and has eigenvalues of $-1 \pm \sqrt{5}$: a saddle point. At $\left(-\frac{2}{3}, -\frac{2}{3}\right)$ the Jacobian is:

$$\begin{bmatrix} -4 & 2 \\ 2 & -2 \end{bmatrix} \tag{15.15}$$

with eigenvalues of $-3 \pm \sqrt{5}$: a stable proper node.

To investigate the region of attraction for $\left(-\frac{2}{3}, -\frac{2}{3}\right)$, consider the level curves of $F = y^2 - x^3 - 2xy$ (see Figure (15.5)).

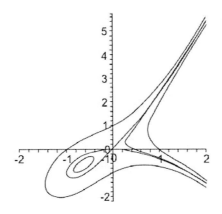

Figure 15.5

The fish shaped, self-intersecting curve is the level curve $F = 0$; the curves around the "head" of the fist are $f > 0$; those out from the "tail" of the fist, and the closed loops, are for $F < 0$; the dot inside the loop is at $\left(-\dfrac{2}{3}, -\dfrac{2}{3}\right)$, a local minimum of F.

The region contained in the closed loop of the fish-shaped curve is certainly part of the region of attraction for $\left(-\dfrac{2}{3}, -\dfrac{2}{3}\right)$. Since $\dfrac{dF}{dt}$ is bounded away from zero away from the critical point, any trajectory must hit the $F = 0$ curve somewhere (F must pass through zero). Those that hit on the closed loop portion approach the critical point; those that hit on the tail portion become unbounded as F decreases without bound. The dividing case is the pair of trajectories that hit the curve exactly at (0,0): the stable separatrices for the saddle point.

Another use for Liapunov functions is when the linearization is ambiguous, such as a center, or one eigenvalue equal to zero.

When a Liapunov function can be found, the function; and particularly the level curves give a great deal of information about solutions and the regions of attraction for the stable critical points.

Exercises

15.1 A   2x2 system

$$\frac{dx}{dt} = f(x, y)$$

$$\frac{dy}{dt} = g(x, y)$$

is a gradient system if and only if $\dfrac{\partial f}{\partial y} = \dfrac{\partial g}{\partial x}$.

Prove this.

What can you tell about solutions to the following gradient systems?

15.2 $\dfrac{dx}{dt} = \begin{bmatrix} 4x(y-x^2) - \sin(x) \\ 2(x^2 - y) \end{bmatrix}.$

15.3 $\dfrac{dx}{dt} = \begin{bmatrix} -x+y-2(x+y)(x+y-2) \\ -y+x-2(x+y)(x+y-2) \end{bmatrix}.$

15.4 $\dfrac{dx}{dt} = \begin{bmatrix} -4x(x^2+y^2+z^2+1) \\ -4y(x^2+y^2+z^2+1) \\ -4z(x^2+y^2+z^2+1) \end{bmatrix}.$

(Hint: the Liapunov function is a function of $r = \sqrt{x^2+y^2+z^2}$).

15.5 Find the critical point(s). What does linearization tell you? This is a gradient system. What does the Liapunov function tell you?

$$\frac{dx}{dt} = -e^x + 1 - 2y$$

$$\frac{dy}{dt} = -2x - 4y - y^2.$$

Plot level curves numerically if necessary.

15.6 Repeat Exercise 15.5 for

$$\frac{dx}{dt} = x^3 - x + y$$

$$\frac{dy}{dt} = x - y.$$

PART III

DISCRETE MODELS

Reproductive Curves

The models we have considered thus far have been of continuous processes. When studying population dynamics, we thought of the population as growing at a steady rate, dependent only on the present population size. Many animals, however, mate and give birth only at particular times of year. For such populations, a discrete sequence of population sizes, measured each generation, might be more appropriate than a continuous function.

For an actual animal species there are several steps a population goes through: breeding, birth, weaning, survival to adulthood, finding a mate; or in insects: eggs, larvae, pupae, adults. For a simple model we can combine these effects into one function.

If we let P_n equal the population at the time of the nth generation, then our model will be of the form

$$P_{n+1} = f(P_n), \tag{16.1}$$

where f incorporates all the changes in population size from one generation to the next; f will always be ≥ 0. If $f(P) < P$, more individuals die in that time period than are born.

A solution to a problem like (16.1) would be a function of n and P_0, such as

$$P_n = g(n, P_0). \tag{16.2}$$

Of course, $g(n, P_0) = \overset{f \text{ composed with itself n times}}{f(f(f \cdots f(P_0) \cdots))} \equiv f^{on}(P_0),$ but sometimes one

can get g in closed form. For instance, if $f(P) = rP, r$ a constant, we get $P_n = r^n P_0$.

Usually we cannot get $g(n, P_0)$ in any useful form. What we really want to know, as in the continuous models, is what happens to the population in the long run. Continuous models could approach a constant, approach a periodic solution, or become unbounded. Our discrete models can also exhibit all of these behaviors, as well as some other possibilities.

One way of analyzing the behavior of P_n, as n gets large, is to consider the graph of $f(P_n)$ or P_{n+1} versus P_n. Graph f, then find P_0 on the horizontal axis. Go up to the curve; the vertical distance is P_1. Now we need to transfer the vertical distance to the horizontal axis, so that we can repeat the process and get P_2. An easy way to accomplish this transfer, is to add the $45°$ line $(x = y)$ to the graph. Move horizontally from (P_0, P_1) to (P_1, P_1), then down to the axis. Repeat. (See figure 16.1).

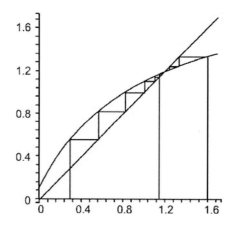

Figure 16.1

In fact, we need only move vertically to f, horizontally to $x = y$, vertically to f, horizontally to $x = y$, etc.

Anywhere the f curve crosses the $x = y$ line is a fixed point; $P_0 = P_1 = P_2 = \cdots$. A great range of types of solutions are possible: stable and unstable fixed points, more than one possible limit, unlimited growth, periodic solutions of period 2 or more generations. The easiest way to see these is to consider some illustrations. Try drawing f and $x = y$ for each of these and doing them yourself.

In figure 16.1 we have a single fixed point P_*. If $0 < P_0 < P_*$ the solution increases monotonically to P_*; if $P_0 > P_*$ the solution decreases monotonically to $P*$.

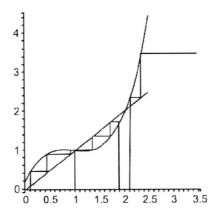

Figure 16.2

Here in figure 16.2 we have two fixed points. If $0 < P_0 < P_{*2}$, the solution approaches P_{*1}. If $P_0 > P_{*2}$, the solution grows without bound.

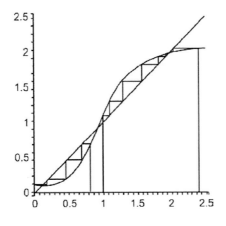

Figure 16.3

In figure 16.3, P_{*1} and P_{*3} are stable; P_{*2} is unstable. If $0 < P_0 < P_{*2}$ solutions tend to P_{*1}. If $P_0 > P_{*2}$, solutions tend to P_{*3}.

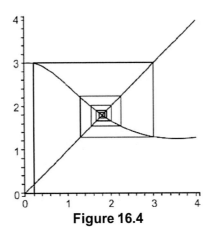

Figure 16.4

In figure 16.4 all solutions approach P_*, but not monotonely; they oscillate.

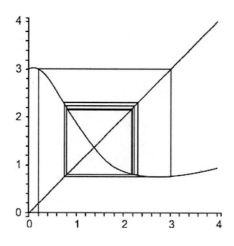

Figure 16.5

In figure 16.5, solutions do not tend to the static point P_*; they tend to a periodic solution of P_a, P_b, P_a, P_b, etc.

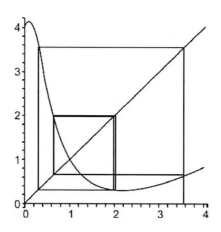

Figure 16.6

Figure 16.6 has a four-generation cycle; start at P_a get $P_b, P_c, P_d, P_a, P_b, P_c$, etc.

Given a fixed point $p*$ (a solution of $f(P) = P$), we would like to determine which sort of fixed point it is.

Theorem 16.1

Let $f : W \subset \mathbb{R} \to W$ be continuously differentiable. Define the sequence $\{x_n\}$ by $x_{n+1} = f(x_n)$. If $x^* \in W$ satisfies $f(x^*) = x^*$ and

(i) $\left| \dfrac{df}{dx}(x^*) \right| < 1$, then x^* is asymptotically stable; $\forall x_0 \in W$

sufficiently close to $x*$, $\lim\limits_{n\to\infty} x_n = x*$.

(ii) $\left|\dfrac{df}{dx}(x*)\right| > 1$, then $x*$ is unstable; $\forall x_j \in W$ sufficiently close to

$x*, \left|x*-x_{j+1}\right| > \left|x*-x_j\right|$.

If $\dfrac{df}{dx}(x*) = 1$, the test fails.

Proof

(i) Let $\left|\dfrac{df}{dx}(x*)\right| = c < 1$. Choose $c < d < 1$. Since

$\lim\limits_{\varepsilon\to 0}\left|\dfrac{f(x*+\varepsilon)-f(x*)}{\varepsilon}\right| = c$, there is a $\delta > 0$ such that for

$|\varepsilon| < \delta, |f(x*+\varepsilon)-f(x*)| < d|\varepsilon|$. Thus if

$|x*-x_0| < \delta, |f(x_0)-f(x*)| = |x_1 - x*| < d|x_0 - x*|$. By induction

$|x_n - x*| < d^n|x_0 - x*|$, so $\lim\limits_{n\to\infty} x_n = x*$.

(ii) Let $\left|\dfrac{df}{dx}(x*)\right| = c > 1$. Choose $c > d > 1$. Since

$\lim\limits_{\varepsilon\to 0} x_n \left|\dfrac{f(x*+\varepsilon)-f(x*)}{\varepsilon}\right| = c$, there is a $\delta > 0$ such that for

$|\varepsilon| > \delta, |f(x*+\varepsilon)-f(x*)| > d|\varepsilon|$. Thus if

$|x*-x_0| < \delta, |f(x_0)-f(x*)| = |x_1 - x*| > d|x_0 - x*| > |x_0. - x*|$.

We cannot, in the second case, say that the sequence continues to get further from $x*$; it may come arbitrarily close further out in the sequence.

A negative slope at a fixed point produces oscillations (such as in figures 16.4 or 16.5); a positive slope produces monotone behavior.

As an example, let us consider

$$f : [0,1] \to [0,1], \quad f(x) = \frac{7}{9}x + x^2 - x^3. \tag{16.3}$$

First we look for fixed points: $f(x) = x$ gives $\frac{7}{9}x + x^2 - x^3 = x$, which in turn gives

$$x^3 - x^2 + \frac{2}{9}x = 0 \tag{16.4}$$

This has roots $x = 0, \frac{1}{3}, \frac{2}{3}$. $\frac{df}{dx} = \frac{7}{9} + 2x - 3x^2$, so $\frac{df}{dx}(0) = \frac{7}{9}, \frac{df}{dx}\left(\frac{1}{3}\right) = \frac{10}{9}$, and $\frac{df}{dx}\left(\frac{2}{3}\right) = \left(\frac{7}{9}\right)$. Thus 0 and $\frac{2}{3}$ are stable, $\frac{1}{3}$ is unstable. Examining the graph,

(see figure 16.7)

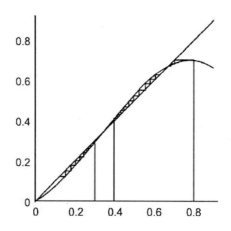

Figure 16.7

We see that for all $x_0 > \frac{1}{3}, x_n$ approaches $\frac{2}{3}$. For $x_0 < \frac{1}{3}, x_n$ approaches 0. This phenomenon is known as a threshold value.

As another example, consider

$$f : [0,1] \to [0,1], f(x) = \frac{10}{3}x(1-x) \tag{16.5}$$

The fixed points are 0 and $\frac{7}{10}, \frac{df}{dx} = \frac{10}{3} - \frac{20}{3}x$, so $\frac{df}{dx}(0) = \frac{10}{3}, \frac{df}{dx}\left(\frac{7}{10}\right) = -\frac{4}{3}$.
Both fixed points are unstable.

Numerical experimentation suggests that the sequence $[x_n]$ settles down to a point oscillation between .4697 and .8303. To show this analytically we use the following:

Remark A point $x*$ is part of a n-periodic solution to a model of the form (16.1) if and only if $x*$ is a fixed point of f^{on}, f composed with itself n times.

Thus a two periodic solution of 16.5 must be defined by a fixed point of

$$f^{02} = f(f) = \frac{10}{3}\left[\frac{10}{3}x(1-x)\right]\left[1 - \frac{10}{3}x(1-x)\right] \tag{16.6}$$

$$= \frac{100}{9}x(1-x)\left(1 - \frac{10}{3}x + \frac{10}{3}x^2\right).$$

Theorem 16.1 can now be used to determine stability of the periodic solution.

Exercises:

16.1 Find and analyze the stability of the fixed points of (16.6). (Hint: a fixed point of f is also a fixed point of f^{02}).

For exercises 16.2-16.4 find and analyze the stability of the fixed points. Sketch the graph.

16.2 $f(x) = 2x(1-x)$.

16.3 $f(x) = \frac{5x^2}{1+x^2}$.

16.4 $f(x) = \frac{2x^2}{1+x^3}$.

16.5 Let $x_0 = a$ and define $x_{n+1} = a^{x_n}$. For what values of a does this have a stable fixed point? What is it?

CHAPTER

Higher Dimensional Fixed points

For many populations, the idea of measuring the total population at each generation is too simple. The age structure of the population, or different birth and death rates for the sexes, may be important. Sometimes a particular subclass (or subclasses) of a population is of interest, such as those with some infectious disease. These can still be treated as a sequence of populations, but now at each step we have a vector representing the population in the different categories.

$$P_{n+1} = F(P_n) \tag{17.1}$$

Perhaps the simplest such models are ones with per capita birth and death rates constant for each different age class. For instance, consider an animal that does not give birth until age two, and has an average litter size of 3 from age 2 through 5; 5 is the maximum age. If we take an all-female model, and assume an equal sex ratio, we get for female birth rate:

$$b_0 = b_1 = 0, b_2 = \cdots b_5 = 1.5 \tag{17.2}$$

Suppose now that the probability of surviving from birth to age 1 of 0.4; from 1 to 2, 0.6; after age 2 the probability of survival each year is 0.8; the probability of surviving from age 5 to age 6 is 0. Taking these death rates and letting $P_n(k)$ be the number of female individuals of age k in the nth generation, we have

$$P_{n+1}(1) = .4P_n(0), P_{n+1}(2) = .6P_n(1), P_{n+1}(3) = .8P_n(2),$$

$$P_{n+1}(4) = .8P_n(3), P_{n+1}(5) = .8P_n(4).$$

The birth rates give us $P_{n+1}(0) = 1.5(P_n(2) + P_n(3) + P_n(4) + P_n(5))$. Putting this all in matrix form gives us

$$P_{n+1} = \begin{bmatrix} 0 & 0 & 1.5 & 1.5 & 1.5 & 1.5 \\ .4 & 0 & 0 & 0 & 0 & 0 \\ 0 & .6 & 0 & 0 & 0 & 0 \\ 0 & 0 & .8 & 0 & 0 & 0 \\ 0 & 0 & 0 & .8 & 0 & 0 \\ 0 & 0 & 0 & 0 & .8 & 0 \end{bmatrix} P_n. \tag{17.3}$$

If we let (17.3) run numerically, we will see that the population is slowly growing. Since this is a linear problem, it will grow without bound, so eventually our model is unrealistic. However, if we divide at each step by the total population, we see that the ratio of age class sizes settles down to a constant,

$$P = (.48, .19, .11, .09, .07, .06)^T, \tag{17.4}$$

while the population is growing by a factor of approximately 1.0145 each step. In fact, 1.0145 is the eigenvalue of the matrix in (17.3) with the largest magnitude, and the vector in (17.4) is the corresponding eigenvector.

This sort of problem of linear growth in an age structured population, with nonoverlapping generations, is known as a Leslie model. The matrix in (17.3) is a Leslie Matrix.

A modified Leslie matrix is often used as a model for populations where some overlap of generations is allowed. For instance, in many bird populations, the important distinctions are between chick, juveniles, and adults. As an example, let us assume a survival rate of 30% for chick, 70% for juveniles, and 80% for adults. If we have an equal sex ratio, and an average clutch size of 4 young (2 females) per adult female (chicks and juveniles do not reproduce), our model would be

$$\begin{aligned} C_{n+1} &= 2A_n \\ J_{n+1} &= .3C_n \\ A_{n+1} &= .7J_n + .8A_n \end{aligned} \tag{17.5}$$

or

$$\begin{bmatrix} C \\ J \\ A \end{bmatrix}_{n+1} = \begin{bmatrix} 0 & 0 & 2 \\ .3 & 0 & 0 \\ 0 & .7 & .8 \end{bmatrix} \begin{bmatrix} C \\ J \\ A \end{bmatrix}_n \tag{17.6}$$

Again, numerically we see the population is growing, but the ratio of the sizes of the three age classes is approximately a constant.

Nonlinear effects can be added to these models to take into account crowding and other population pressures. For instance, in birds, the juvenile survival rate can be strongly dependent on available nesting sites; if the adult population is high, there will be fewer open sites, and thus a lower juvenile survival rate. If we change the juvenile survival rate in our previous example to

$.7\left(1-\dfrac{A_n}{300}\right)$ to reflect this, we get

$$C_{n+1} = 2A_n$$
$$J_{n+1} = .3C_n$$
$$A_{n+1} = .7J_n\left(1-\dfrac{An}{300}\right)+.8A_n.$$

(17.7)

This system has a fixed point at (314.3, 94.3, 157.1). Numerically, it appears stable. To analyze this question, we need a higher dimensional equivalent of Theorem 16.1.

Theorem 17.1

Let F be a continuously differentiable function taking a subset of $\mathbb{R}^n$ into itself: $F:U \rightarrow U$. If $x^* \in U$ is a fixed point, $F(x^*) = x^*$, let $J(x^*)$ be the Jacobian of F evaluated at x^*. If

(i)   All of the eigenvalues of $J(x^*)$ are less than one in absolute value, then x^* is an asymptotically stable fixed point.

(ii)   One or more of the eigenvalues are greater than one in absolute value, then x^* is an unstable fixed point.

(iii)   One or more of the eigenvalues are equal to one in absolute value and all others are less, the test fails.

The proof is similar to the proof of (16.1). For x sufficiently close to x^*,

$$F(x) = F(x^*) + J(x^*)(x-x^*) + h = x^* + J(x^*)(x-x^*) + h,$$

where h is order $(x-x^*)^2$ and can be made arbitrarily small. If all of the eigenvalues of $J(x^*)$ are smaller than one, under an appropriate norm $\|J(x^*)(x-x^*)\| < \|x-x^*\|$. Thus, $F(x)$ is closer to x^* than x was.

In our example $J(x^*) = J(314,94,157)$ is

$$\begin{bmatrix} 0 & 0 & 2 \\ .3 & 0 & 0 \\ 0 & .367 & .58 \end{bmatrix}. \tag{17.8}$$

The characteristic equation is

$$\lambda^3 - .58\lambda^2 - .22 = 0, \tag{17.9}$$

and numerically we find the eigenvalues to be 0.870395 and $0.145198 \pm 0.481327i$. These have magnitudes of 0.870395 and 0.50275. Thus the fixed point (314,94,157) is stable.

Another problem often modeled this way is the spread of an epidemic. A simple model of a contagious disease might divide the population up into susceptibles, infecteds, and recovereds. A common model for transmission of a disease says that the probability of a susceptible catching the disease from a given infected during some time period, is a constant, p. Thus the probability of not catching the disease in the time period is $(1-p)^I$, where I is the number of infecteds. We can write this as e^{-aI}, for some $a > 0$. Let b equal the fraction of infecteds that recover in the given time period, and c be the fraction of recovereds that lose their immunity and become susceptible again (this could be 0 for diseases where immunity is permanent). This gives us the model

$$s_{n+1} = e^{-aI_n}S_n + cR_n$$
$$I_{n+1} = (1 - e^{-aI_n})s_n + (1-b)I_n$$
$$R_{n+1} = bI_n + (1-c)R_n.$$

It can readily be seen, that for many choices of parameters, solutions settle down to a constant level of infection in the population.

Much more complicated models can be built, though they must usually be studied numerically, rather than analytically. In some diseases (such as measles in school children), contact, and thus the transmission of the disease, are periodic rather than constant throughout the year. In many situations, particularly in modeling small variables and running the simulation many times, expected population size, probability of extinction within the next hundred years, and other information can be obtained.

Exercises

17.1 Determine the stable age distribution and the growth rate for the example given in (17.5).

17.2 Suppose that crowding affects egg production instead of juvenile survival. Analyze the model you obtained from (17.5) by changing the average number of female chicks produced per breeding female from 2 to $2\left(1-\dfrac{A_n}{500}\right)$.

17.3 Analyze

$$A_{n+1} = 2B_n\left(1-\frac{B_n}{1000}\right)$$

$$B_{n+1} = .7A_n\left(1-\frac{B_n}{500}\right)+.8B_n.$$

17.4 In the example given in (17.10), let $b=1$. Analyze the stability of the $I=0, R=0$ steady state. Choose parameters such that this trivial solution is not stable. Analyze this problem.

CHAPTER

The Mathematics of Sickle Cell Anemia

Sickle cell anemia is basically a standard Mendelian dominant-recessive trait, with sickle cell being the recessive trait. Since people who have the disease rarely, if ever, reach reproductive age, one might expect sickle cell anemia to have died out of the gene pool many generations ago. A fairly simple mathematical model gives us some insight into the situation, and gives an explanation, both of why the disease persists, and for why in this country, it is chiefly found in African Americans and South Sea Islanders.

Sickle cell is a one locus, two-allele trait. This means that for a particular location (locus) on the chromosome strand, there are two possible genes; let us call them A and a. This leads to three possible genotypes when two gametes combine to form an individual. Both gametes could have an A gene at the locus we are interested in, or both could have a, or one could have A and the other a. Thus, we could have AA, Aa, or aa. The two unmixed types, AA and aa, are called homozygotes; Aa is the heterozygote. In certain traits, one of the genes (say A) is dominant. This means that the AA and the Aa genotypes appear the same; we say they form a phenotype. The other phenotype is the recessive aa. Sickle cell is a trait of this nature: those with the recessive trait have the disease. This means that people who do not have sickle cell may still be heterozygotes, thus carrying the a gene.

Now, let us set up the mathematical model. We will treat generations as being discrete rather than using a continuous time scale. Let D_n be the number of AA in the nth generation, $2H_n$ be the number of Aa (the 2 makes life a bit easier later on), and R_n be the number of aa. We do not actually want to deal with these quantities, but we will need them to set up the problem. We will actually be working with g_n, the fraction of the gene pool in the nth generation that is A, some number between 0 and 1. We will try to get a relationship between g_n and g_{n+1}.

Let us assume that the gene distribution is the same in the male and female populations, and that there is no preference shown for one genotype or another in selecting a mate. The gene pool at the time of the nth generation had g_n A's and $(1-g_n)a$'s. The probability of two A gametes mating is g_n^2, the probability of A gamete and an a gamete mating is $2g_n (1-g_n)$, and for two a's, $(1-g_n)^2$. This if N_n is the population size at the time of the nth generation, we have

$$D_n = g_n^2 N_n$$
$$2Hn = 2g_n(1-g)N_n$$
$$R_n = (1-g_n)^2 N_n \qquad\qquad (18.1)$$

Now, we wish to compute g_{n+1}, the fraction A of the gene pool at the $(n+1)$ st generation. First, we need to figure out how many of the *nth* generation survive to reproductive age. In general, the survival rates would be functions of $D_n, 2H_n$, and R_n, and these functions could be of various forms. For our purposes, we will assume that the survival rates are linear. Thus

rD_n : Number of AA available for reproduction at the time of the

$(n+1)$ st generation

$s2H_n$: Number of Aa available

tR_n : Number of aa available

where r,s, and t are constants between 0 and 1.

We assume that all surviving individuals have equal likelihood of contributing to the gene pool. Each AA individual contributes two A genes, each Aa one (and one a gene), and the aa individuals contribute no A genes. Thus, the number of A genes in the pool will be $\alpha[2(rD_n)+1(s2H_n)]$, where α is the likelihood of an individual contributing. The total gene pool will be two from each contributing individual:

$$\alpha[2(rD_n)+2(s2H_n)+2(tR_n)]. \qquad\qquad (18.2)$$

Thus, we get:

$$g_{n+1} = \frac{rD_n + sH_n}{rD_n + 2sH_n + tR_n} \qquad\qquad (18.3)$$

or, substituting (18.1) into (18.3), and canceling N_n,

$$g_{n+1} = \frac{r(g_n)^2 + sg_n(1-g_n)}{r(g_n)^2 + 2sg_n(1-g_n) + t(1-g_n)^2}. \qquad\qquad (18.4)$$

What we have done to this point holds true for any one locus, two allele trait. Now, let us use some of what we know about sickle cell anemia. People with the disease essentially do not reach reproductive age, so t, the aa survival rate, is zero. Substituting this into (18.4) and canceling a g_n, gives

$$g_{n+1} = \frac{rg_n + s(1 - g_n)}{rg_n + 2s(1 - g_n)}.$$ (18.5)

This gives us a map $g_{n+1} = f(g_n)$. To determine what happens to g_n as n approaches ∞, we must first look for any fixed points, i.e., values such that $f(g) = g$. Setting $g_{n+1} = g_n = g$ in (18.5) and simplifying, we get:

$$(r - 2s)g^2 + (3s - r)g - s = 0$$ (18.6)

This factors to $[(r - 2s)g + s](g - 1)$, so we have two roots:

$$g = 1 \text{ and } g = \frac{s}{(2s - r)} = \frac{s}{(s + (s - r))}.$$

If $r \geq s$, then the second root will be ≥ 1, which takes it out of the realistic range for g. Thus, with only one fixed point at $g = 1$ and $\dfrac{df}{dg} > 0$ $\left(\text{where } \dfrac{df}{dg} = \dfrac{rs}{(2s + (r - 2s))^2}\right)$, we find the g approaches 1 as n increases, and the population settles down to all AA (See Figure 18.1).

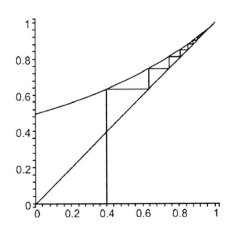

Figure 18.1

However, if $s > r$, then $0 < \dfrac{s}{(s + (s - r))} < 1$, and we get another possible

solution. In fact, $\dfrac{df}{dg} > 0$ is enough to guarantee that $\dfrac{s}{(2s - r)}$, and not 1, is the stable fixed point (see Figure 18.2), so the problem settles down, with $gn < 1$; thus, the a gene persists.

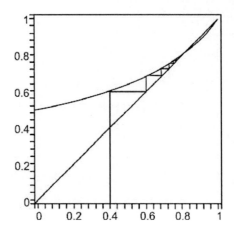

Figure 18.2

Is there any reason the survival of heterozygotes would be higher? It turns out that the red blood cells of Aa individuals, while not as misshapen as those of individuals with sickle cell, are shaped enough differently that they are resistant to malaria. This is why we see sickle cell in populations that evolved in the presence of malaria and not in others.

Exercises:

18.1 In this country, the malaria pressure has been removed. Sickle cell anemia should be evolving out of the American Black population. With $s = r$, suppose $g_0 = .95$. What will be the value of g_5?

18.2 What must the ratio of s to r be for $g=.95$ to be a stable fixed point?

18.3 Find $\dfrac{df}{dg}$ at the fixed points for (18.5) and analyze the three cases:

$$s < r, s = r, s > r.$$

18.4 Suppose that for some one locus-two allele trait the homozygotes have equal survival rates, but the heterozygote has zero survival. Analyze.

18.5 Repeat Exercise 18.4 if the homozygotes have different, but non-zero survival rates, and the heterozygote still has zero survival.

18.6 What happens to the population if a trait has no effect on survival, i.e., $r = s = t$?

CHAPTER

Chaos

In Chapter 16 we saw examples of sequences of the form

$$x_{n+1} = f(x_n) \tag{19.1}$$

that were unbounded, others that converged to a point, and others with periodic solutions of period two or higher. These do not, however, represent all the possibilities. As an example, let us consider the sequence given by

$$x_{n+1} = f(x_n) = \alpha x_n (1 - x_n), \tag{19.2}$$

where α is a constant to be specified. If $0 < \alpha < 4$, f will map the unit interval into itself.

First, set α equal to $\dfrac{3}{2}$ and choose an x_0 in $(0,1)$. The sequence converges to $\dfrac{1}{3}$. For instance, with $x_0 = \dfrac{1}{2}$, we get

$$x_0 = .5, x_1 = .375, x_2 = .351563, x_3 = .341949, x_4 = .33753, x_5$$
$$= .335404, x_6 = .334363, \cdots, x_{10} = .333397, \cdots \tag{19.3}$$

Since $f'\left(\dfrac{1}{3}\right) = \dfrac{1}{2}$, theorem (16.1) tells us that $\dfrac{1}{3}$ is a stable fixed point.

With $\alpha = \dfrac{5}{2}, x_0 = .5$, we get

$$x_0 = .5, x_1 = .625, x_2 = .585938, x_3 = .606537, \cdots, x_{10} = .599948, x_{11} = .600026 \tag{19.4}$$

As we can check, .6 is a fixed point, and $f'(.6) = -\dfrac{1}{2}$, and theorem (16.1) again tells us that the fixed point is stable.

For $\alpha = 3.2$, we get a sequence that settles down to a period-two oscillation between approximately .799455 and .5103045; $\alpha = 3.5$ gives a period-four solution: .826941, .500885, .874997, and .38282.

For $\alpha = 3.9$, however, the sequence given by (19.2) does not appear to settle down at all. Graphing f, and iterating seems to give a sequence of points dense in the interval $\left(\dfrac{1}{3.9}, \dfrac{3.9}{4}\right)$. This is an example of a chaotic solution.

A well known result due to Tien-Yien Li and James Yorke (see T.Y. Li and J.A. Yorke, *Period three implies chaos*, American Mathematics Monthly, <u>82</u> no. 10 (Dec. 1975), pp. 985-992) will help us understand this phenomenon.

Theorem 19.1

Let f be a continuous function taking an interval J into itself. Suppose there exists an $a \in J$ such that

$$f^{03}(a) \le a < f(a) < f^{02}(a) \ \text{ or } \ f^{03}(a) \ge a > f(a) > f^{02}(a) \quad (19.5)$$

(Any function with a period-three point satisfies one or the other of these conditions.) Then for every positive integer k there is an $x_0 \in J$ such that the sequence $x_0, x_1, x_2, \cdots$ generated by (19.1) is $k-$ periodic.

Proof

Assume $f^{03}(a) \le a < f(a) < f^{02}(a)$. Let $J_0 = \big(a, f(a)\big), J_1 = \big(f(a), f^2(a)\big)$. For a given $k > 1$, define a sequence of intervals I_i by $I_0 = J_0, I_1 = I_2 = \cdots I_{k-1} = J_1$ and $I_{n+k} = I_n$. (Thus, this is a k- periodic sequence of intervals.) By the continuity of f, $J_1 \subseteq f(J_0)$, and since $f^{03}(a) \le a$, we have $\big(J_0 \cup J_1\big) \subseteq f(J_1)$. Now define a nested sequence of intervals, Q_n, such that

$$f^{on}(Q_n) = I_n. \tag{19.6}$$

Let $Q_0 = I_0$. Clearly, $f^0(Q_0) = I_0$. If $f^{o(n-1)}(Q_{n-1}) = I_{n-1}$, then

$$I_n \subseteq f(I_{n-1}) = f\left(f^{o(n-1)}(Q_{n-1})\right) = f^{on}(Q_{n-1}).$$

By continuity of f^{on}, there is a compact interval $Q_n \subseteq Q_{n-1}$, such that $f^{on}(Q_n) = I_n$. Thus, we have defined the sequence $\{Q_n\}$ inductively. Now, $f^{ok}(Q_k) = I_k \supset Q_k$, so f^{ok} has a fixed point in Q_k; that is, x^*. If x^* is a fixed point of f^{ok}, it is a periodic point of period k for f. Furthermore, since x^* is in Q_j for all $j \leq k$, $f^{oj}(x^*)$ is in I_j for all j. Thus x^* is not a periodic point of any period less than k, since $x^* = f^{ok}(x^*)$ is in J_0, but $f^{oj}(x^*)$ is in J_1 for all $0 < j < k$. This completes the proof.

The proof for $f^{o3}(a) \geq a > f(a) > f^{o2}(a)$ is similar. This theorem can easily be extended to the following:

Theorem 19.2

Let f, J_0 and J_1 be as above. For any sequence of positive integers, $\{a_n\}$ there is a choice of x_0 in I_0, such that the sequence defined by (19.1) is in J_1 for a_1 iterations, then in J_0 for one, then J_2 for a_2 iterations, then J_0 for one, and so forth. This means there are non-periodic sequences that never approach a periodic sequence.

Proof

Define the sequence of intervals I_1 by
$$I_0 = J_0, I_1 = I_2 = \cdots = I_{a1} = J_1, I_{a1+1} = J_0, I_{a1+2} = \cdots = I_{a1+a2+1} = J_1, I_{a1+a2+2} = J_0, \text{etc}$$

Now define the sequence of intervals $Q_n s$ as before. Let $Q = \bigcap_{n=0}^{\infty} Q_n$. Since Q is the intersection of a nested sequence of compact sets, it is not empty. Any $x \in Q$ is in $Q_n \forall n$, so $f^{on}(x) \in f^{on}(Q_n) = I_n$.

The existence of periodic points of infinitely many different periods was sometimes used as a definition of chaos, although it is not the modern definition. Using any non-periodic sequence in theorem 19.2 (such as $a_1 = 1, 2, 3, \cdots$), we can construct sequences generated by (19.1) that never remain close to any periodic sequence. Also, the periodic points are so scattered through the interval, that arbitrarily small differences in initial conditions can put you on periodic sequences of completely different periods or a non-periodic sequence. Asymptotic behavior is not even a piecewise continuous function of initial conditions.

Other functions can give different results. Some functions have regions such that any x_0 in them leads to a convergent sequence, but other points that give rise to non-convergent sequences. One such function is

$$f(x) \begin{cases} 3x & 0 \le x \le \dfrac{1}{3} \\[2mm] 1 & \dfrac{1}{3} < x < \dfrac{1}{2} \\[2mm] \dfrac{1}{2} & x = \dfrac{1}{2} \\[2mm] 0 & \dfrac{1}{2} < x < \dfrac{2}{3} \\[2mm] 3x - 2 & \dfrac{2}{3} \le x \le 1 \end{cases}$$ (19.7)

This function is displayed in Figure 19.1. The set of points for which the sequence defined by the above function does not converge is a Cantor set (see D.R. Arterburn and W.D. Stone, A Cantor set of nonconvergence. American Mathematical Monthly, 96 No. 7 (Aug-Sept 1989), pp.604-608).

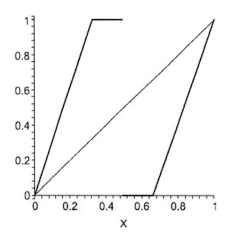

Figure 19.1

Similar results are possible for mapping of the plane into itself, or higher dimensions. The regions of convergence, and the chaotic points can be quite complicated. For some strange and beautiful pictures of this, see The Beauty of Fractal, (H.-O. Peitgen and P.H. Richter, the beauty of fractals: images of complex dynamical systems, Springer Verlag, 1986).

Exercises

19.1 Find the interval for α in equation (19.2), such that of $f^{\circ 2}$ has a stable fixed point that is not a fixed point of f.

19.2 Consider the function given in equation (19.7).

(a) Write a number in the interval $(0,1)$ in base three (i.e.,

$$X = \frac{a_1}{3} + \frac{a_2}{3^2} + \cdots + \frac{a_j}{3^j} + \cdots)$$ and determine the effect of f.

(b) Find the sequence given by $x_0 = \dfrac{9}{13}$ (Hint work in base three).

(c) Can you describe (in terms of the base three representation) the set of points that are not mapped to a fixed point?